"The Object Lesson[s]... to magic: the book[s] and animate them[...] political struggle, [...] Filled with fascina[ting...] accessible prose, the books make the everyday world come to life. Be warned: once you've read a few of these, you'll start walking around your house, picking up random objects, and musing aloud: 'I wonder what the story is behind this thing?'"

Steven Johnson, author of *Where Good Ideas Come From* and *How We Got to Now*

"Object Lessons describes themselves as 'short, beautiful books,' and to that, I'll say, amen. . . . If you read enough Object Lessons books, you'll fill your head with plenty of trivia to amaze and annoy your friends and loved ones—caution recommended on pontificating on the objects surrounding you. More importantly, though . . . they inspire us to take a second look at parts of the everyday that we've taken for granted. These are not so much lessons about the objects themselves, but opportunities for self-reflection and storytelling. They remind us that we are surrounded by a wondrous world, as long as we care to look."

John Warner, *The Chicago Tribune*

OBJECT LESSONS

A book series about the hidden lives of ordinary things.

Series Editors:

Ian Bogost and Christopher Schaberg

In association with

BOOKS IN THE SERIES

mushroom

SARA RICH

BLOOMSBURY ACADEMIC
NEW YORK · LONDON · OXFORD · NEW DELHI · SYDNEY

BLOOMSBURY ACADEMIC
Bloomsbury Publishing Inc
1385 Broadway, New York, NY 10018, USA
50 Bedford Square, London, WC1B 3DP, UK
29 Earlsfort Terrace, Dublin 2, Ireland

BLOOMSBURY, BLOOMSBURY ACADEMIC and the Diana logo are trademarks of
Bloomsbury Publishing Plc

First published in the United States of America 2023

Bloomsbury Publishing Inc does not have any control over, or responsibility for, any third-
party websites referred to or in this book. All internet addresses given in this book were
correct at the time of going to press. The author and publisher regret any inconvenience
caused if addresses have changed or sites have ceased to exist, but can accept no
responsibility for any such changes.

Whilst every effort has been made to locate copyright holders the publishers would be
grateful to hear from any person(s) not here acknowledged.

Library of Congress Cataloging-in-Publication Data
Names: Rich, Sara A., author.
Title: Mushroom / Sara Rich.
Description: New York: Bloomsbury Academic, 2023. | Series: Object lessons | Includes
bibliographical references and index. | Summary: "Explores an object that is both magical
and medicinal, that nurtures ancient traditions, that is the object of foragers', cooks', and
scientists' attention, and which has properties that continue to baffle physicians and
psychiatrists"– Provided by publisher.
Identifiers: LCCN 2022026371 (print) | LCCN 2022026372 (ebook) | ISBN 9781501386589
(paperback) | ISBN 9781501386596 (epub) | ISBN 9781501386602 (pdf) |
ISBN 9781501386619 (ebook other)
Subjects: LCSH: Mushrooms.
Classification: LCC QK617 .R47 2023 (print) | LCC QK617 (ebook) |
DDC 579.6–dc23/eng/20220622

LC record available at https://lccn.loc.gov/2022026371
LC ebook record available at https://lccn.loc.gov/2022026372

ISBN: PB: 978-1-5013-8658-9
ePDF: 978-1-5013-8660-2
eBook: 978-1-5013-8659-6

Series: Object Lessons

Typeset by Deanta Global Publishing Services, Chennai, India
Printed and bound in the United States of America

To find out more about our authors and books visit www.bloomsbury.com and
sign up for our newsletters.

To my parents

CONTENTS

PART V MAGIC 85

PRE-AMBLE

You are about to embark on a foraging venture. You will wind through forests and ecotones, and in your wanderings, you will find many mushrooms—some medicinal or magical, others powerfully metaphorical. Where we're going, the brush may be dense at times, but press on: we're not in a rush, and eventually, we will come full circle. But before we begin methodically treading along this tangled loop trail, maybe it's worth asking: what does it mean to forage?

In Frédéric Gros' *A Philosophy of Walking*, so many types of ambulation are considered, parsed, exemplified, and qualified. City strolls, mountain rambles, woodland hikes, they are all given philosophical precedence.[1] He weaves the reader through these various paths, yet the act of foraging along them might use some further exposition.

Both forage and foray developed from the Old French *forrer*, but over time, they have accumulated slightly different

---

[1]Gros, Frédéric, *A Philosophy of Walking* (London and New York: Verso, 2015).

meanings. To forage is to foray with purpose. When I was young, my mom and I would walk the dirt roads where we lived in rural Kansas to pick up trash from the ditches, which had the dual function of ecological stewardship, and with enough aluminum cans, a small profit to boot. This kind of walking is a complex union of roving and rooting. The forager is on a quest, seeking specific items, like flattened cans of Natty Light, a good deal at a yard sale, or morels in springtime.

Potawatomi botanist and poet Robin Wall Kimmerer writes that when botanists set out into forests and fields looking for plants, they call it a foray. She then suggests that when writers venture off into the wilds, we might call it a *metaphoray*.[2] We might then think of our fungal quest, where ordinary mushrooms turn metaphysical, as a *metaphorage*. If walking can be a way of worlding, as in Zapatista thought, foraging might be a way of folding into the world: allowing oneself to be overwhelmed by the quest, tricked by the whims of that which is sought, satisfied that the destination is uncertain, perhaps never to be found.[3] Sometimes it seems that all of existence is metaphoragic.

[2]Kimmerer, Robin Wall, *Braiding Sweetgrass: Indigenous Wisdom, Scientific Knowledge, and the Teachings of Plants* (Minneapolis: Milkweed Editions, 2013), 46.

[3]Sundberg, Juanita, "Decolonizing posthumanist geographies," *Cultural Geographies* 21.1 (2014): 33-47.

Like most wanderers, I've made the obligatory but pleasurable forays around big cities like Paris, Chicago, Toronto, Athens, and Jerusalem. And of course, I've roamed through Rome. But most of my walking has been of a different, more purposeful, nature. In college, I disassociated myself from Jehovah's Witnesses. Ten years earlier, while my dad was deployed in Saudi Arabia for Desert Storm, my mom and I had converted, and my young siblings soon followed suit. But in my sophomore year of college, I renounced my baptism. My mother, brother, and sister were forced either to shun me or be expelled from the church. The following winter, I set out walking and hitchhiking across New Mexico, seeking a theo-ontological reset. Wonderful as it was, that trek proved insufficient, so I dropped out of college, took my student loan refund check, and trudged solo across Italy and Greece, belongings stuffed into my dad's Navy seabag. Gros might consider these walks to have been melancholic, awakening ghosts from earlier times so that they might be drowned in the alchemy of diluted sorrow.[4] But in the spirit of foraging, something was being sought: if not provisions per se, that thing that one needs in addition to bread alone.

As early mycologist Elias Fries wrote, if one is tall and a good walker and in good health, it's not impossible to walk

---

[4]Gros, *Philosophy of Walking*, 149.

75 kilometers in 12 hours.[5] Over the years since those early treks, I've walked thousands of miles, often twenty or thirty in a day, through upstate New York, all over Mexico, Cyprus, Lebanon, Belgium, the Maltese Islands, the south coast of England, the temperate rainforest of southern Appalachia, and now the cypress swamps of South Carolina. There is always something to seek, something hidden to find. But even more things elude me, and rightly so.

That my parents cultivated the habit of foraging for trash and wild mushrooms incidentally prepared me for survey archaeology too, where slow, deliberate movements and visual scanning of the ground are in pursuit of stone tools rather than toadstools. Picking up a discarded or lost projectile point, scraper or burin, made by ancestors thousands of years ago, makes one feel an intimate echo from the past that reminds us how the bygone is never really gone. I used to ask myself while perusing plowed fields for weeks on end, *Where did I leave it?* Sometimes, something was found right where it'd been left.

There is also a strange ancestral contact made when foraging for wild mushrooms and plants. The ability, known to hunters the world over, to walk into a forest with nothing and come back out with dinner issues a residual pride, felt through the ancient ones looking on in approval that you've

---

[5]Fries, Elias, *Autobiography: Historiola Studii Mei Mycologici* (The Danish Mycological Society: Copenhagen, 1955 [1857]), 145.

managed to avoid losing, so far, that shred of their wisdom. And there is a similarity between stalking and foraging: although the forager's prey isn't on the move, it is elusive, and both practices involve looking carefully for telltale signs of proximity, like favorite plants, the dampness of the soil, scats, tracks, and spore prints.

But as far as mushrooms are concerned, my sense of being awash in the glow of ancestral pride is mostly based on a vivid imagination. My Scandinavian, Germanic, and Anglo-Celtic ancestors were most likely what Valentina and Gordon Wasson would have called mycophobic—afraid of mushrooms.[6] Only my Tsalagi forebears in the mountains of Appalachia would have been mycophilic, now nodding in approval at their granddaughter for finding food in the open air. Across the Atlantic though, we would probably have to go way back to pre-Christian times to find a mycophiliac among them. But if you go back far enough, everyone was a hunter-gatherer, fisher-forager. So let's join them—let's walk.

But know first that for the forager, the end results are never exactly what was anticipated. Sometimes you find nothing. Other times, it's the mother lode. During our pursuit, we might even become like the microscopic hyphae composing fungal mycelia, forging new passages in the dirt and connecting with unlikely kin.

---

[6]Wasson, Valentina Pavlovna and R. Gordon Wasson, *Mushroom: Russia and History* (New York: Pantheon Books, 1957).

SUMMER

Chicken-of-the-woods
Dutch: *zwavelzwam* (sulfur mushroom)
French: *polypore soufré* (sulfurous polypore)
Latin: *Laetiporus sulphureus*

While other languages identify this shelf mushroom by its sulfurous hue, its most common American name betrays its flavor, which seems appropriate for the world's most notorious gourmands. Chicken-of-the-woods is part of a parasitic polypore fungus that usually prefers to attack hardwood trees. Its parasitic nature makes it easier for me to justify harvesting it aggressively.

Most recently, I've gathered chickens on oaks in early May along the Waccamaw River in South Carolina and in mid-June in the Appalachian Mountains of Western North Carolina. However, it first came into my kitchen by way of the woods near Kessel-lo, Belgium, where it appeared regularly in summer and fall. It is a distinctive fungus. Each layered shelf of mushroom is bright orange or yellow and has a soft but sturdy texture. The shelves are often densely stacked like fluffy layers of feathers on a feisty, neon chicken.

Not surprisingly, chicken-of-the-woods makes a delicious meatless substitute for poultry. The texture, density, and flavor are all comparable. The big difference is that you don't have to pluck the fungus, or gut it. In this case, butchering is a bloodless affair. (Annual chicken butchering day was why I abandoned meat at age 12, so I was thrilled to make this mushroom's acquaintance some years ago.) I recommend cutting your harvest into bite-sized pieces to fry, or into finger-sized strips to grill. Like other mushrooms, you can also marinate them before cooking.

Because this mushroom can grow to several pounds in weight, depending on how much you harvest, you may have leftovers. Just freeze them, same as you would with chicken.

Chicken-of-the-woods does cause gastric upset in some, so it is recommended that you eat a small amount first, and then wait a few days before eating more.

PART I

MYSTERY

Destroying Angel

I have been lucky—some might even say blessed, although I'm hesitant to use that word since it denies coincidence and cunning in favor of a "chosen-one" trope. At any rate, not once in my thirty-some years of foraging have I had an adverse reaction to a wild mushroom (knock on wood). I've hunted the choice edibles, like morels and chanterelles, but also the trickier ones, like corals, boletes, agarics, honeys, and puffballs. Ringless honey mushrooms and chicken-of-the-woods cause gastric upset in some, but I can eat them meal after meal and fare just fine.

For the record, I am cautious. My dad's advice is to look for the bugs: if they're eating it, you can too. But to be sure, I avoid the entire *Inocybe* genus of small, poisonous toadstools by heeding the phrase, "little and brown, leave 'em in the ground." Generally, I defer to the guidebooks and the old adage "when in doubt, throw it out"—or better yet, "when in doubt, don't pluck it out."

The use of the pronoun "it" in this maxim is somewhat deceptive though. A mushroom is part of an underground fungal body of mycelium, a creature that flaunts its flesh between the Linnaean kingdoms of animal and vegetable. Fungi are lively organisms whose complex behavior surely warrants the usage of a pronoun that acknowledges agency, intention, and even cognition. But the complications of mycelial gender and sexuality render irrelevant our other English-language pronouns of "she" and "he." Weird fiction writer China Miéville called fungi "the kingdom of the grey" to describe the bizarre nature of these organisms, how they blend rigid boundaries left and right like spores dispersed into air, up and down as through soil and water, into a muddy grisaille palette. No, English pronouns simply won't do.

Proposing that we reconsider using the dismissive 'it' in reference to nonhuman agents, Robin Wall Kimmerer offers the Potawatomi word *ki* as a pronoun to signify a being of the living earth.[1] Although linguistically unrelated, this root

---

[1] Kimmerer, Robin Wall, "Speaking of Nature: Finding a Language that Affirms Our Kinship with the Natural World," *Orion Magazine*, March/April 2017.

has fortuitous resonance with the Germanic word *kin*, which signifies familial relations with others to whom we may or may not be linked genetically. And in humanity's first written language, Sumerian, *ki* means earth, land, or place. It signifies a locus or rootedness that seems appropriate for fungal lifeways. So with a language that acknowledges animacy in more-than-human persons, the adage now becomes "when it doubt, don't pluck *ki* out."

As a child growing up in rural Kansas, spring was morel season. With brown paper bags in tow, we would trudge through the horse pasture into the wooded areas of our property. My family acquired the land in the early 1900s, but before then, it was the Chippewa and Munsee Indian Reservation. Many Munsee still lived there, one of whom, a lovely woman named Cecilia, was my babysitter. Before her displaced ancestors arrived in what would be known as the Chippewa Hills, and before the arrival of white settlers and their mercenaries, the land was home to the Lakota Sioux and, later, the Osage peoples. For hundreds, probably thousands, of years, people have known that dead elm trees were good indicators of where springtime morels might be found. Back then, they used bark or hide bags for gathering. In the 1980s, we used brown paper grocery bags from Ray's IGA. On good days, grocery bags were brimming with wrinkled organs that looked like elongated brains but tasted like no other kind of flesh. On other days, even following a soft warm rain, there was nothing to be seen. Sight unseen, they were still there, their mycelia crawling beneath the horse-manured soil, through hedge roots, buffalo bones, burial grounds, spent ammunition, and broken glass, waiting for the right moment to send sporocarps, or fruiting bodies, through the sandy loam and clay substrate to the surface, where they would spread their spores and make more of their kind. Lucky, or luck-*ki*, for us.

As an adult, my relationship with mushrooms took an unexpected turn. Like some sort of mystical guardian, whenever I needed them most, they were there. After moving from Kansas to Wisconsin for graduate school, my luck had seemed to run out. Penniless, I was close to selling my own eggs or dropping out to join the Navy. After a week of living off black tea and a single bar of chocolate that my grandmother had mailed from Kansas, I was walking with my dog Sophia on the shores of Lake Michigan and stumbled on a patch of wild squash. On the way back to the apartment, backpack stuffed with squash, we cut through Kilbourn-Kadish Park, which was peppered with dozens of delicious meadow mushrooms. My eggs and education remained intact.

Having experienced this particular stroke of luck on the traditional lands of the Potawatomi reinforces the idea of a mushroom as *ki*—somehow knowledgeable, bounteous, maybe even *ki*nd. Now, in South Carolina on the traditional lands of the Waccamaw, I keep following my dad's advice but also that of my friend, Chief Hatcher: wherever you pluck something from the forest, leave a little sage or tobacco in return. I've adopted this practice to honor him, his kin and their ancestors, and this land where I'm a guest, but I'm still backtracking to pay my respects for the bones, fruit, shells, feathers, firewood, rocks, and mushrooms the cypress swamps have provided me over the last few years. Although I no longer forage out of necessity, mushrooming for survival did not end in Potawatomi territory. It's in part for this reason that I try now to be a better guest and give back—because I know what I owe them, and I suspect they do too.

During my doctorate in Belgium, money always seemed to dry up in the fall, fortuitously the time of year when mushrooms flourish. There, foraging assumed a more adventurous nature, as mysterious, unfamiliar varieties within the genera *Coprinus*, *Boletus*, *Agaricus*, *Lyophylum*, and *Ramaria*, were thrown routinely into the cookpot, alongside foraged chestnuts, beechnuts, chives, blackberries, apples, and pears. Eight years in Northern Europe fostered not only foraging skills, but a profound gratitude and even a kind of reverence for mushrooms. Gradually learning their names in Dutch, French, and Latin helped distinguish between the delicacies, the medicinals, and those whose toxins could vanquish enemies or extinguish small armies.

In a place where thousands of women had been condemned to the gallows, rapids, or flames for such knowledge, my ken verged into the esoteric. Many of the languages of Indigenous peoples that animated things like plants, rocks, and mushrooms, shared a fate with the language of sciences forbidden by the clergy—and those practiced by women were deemed all the more demonic, given as we are to consorting with the devil. I needed to exhume these murdered languages and suffocated ways of knowing. Soon I was drawn into antiquarian bookshops—one in particular on Naamsestraat in Leuven—with ancient volumes on witchcraft and alchemy. Yellowed pages with ligatured typeset and exquisite woodcuts smelled like deadly secrets, and I listened closely. Written there in Belgium but set in modern-day Kansas, my first novel's protagonist accidentally kills the Dean of Religious Studies with a concoction of false morels and horse nettle. She is subsequently lynched for witchcraft.

As one awakens to the powers of mushrooms—diverse and perverse—it becomes apparent that these humble, dirty, slimy, and often smelly beings of the earth are hiding something. Between the lamellae, beneath the pileus, there are secrets that whisper of sentience but also insinuate something else, something more. Riddled with chemical compounds that feed, heal, sicken, kill, and vault into altered states of consciousness, mushrooms might be insulted if one were to suggest that they possess godlike qualities of creation and destruction, because what and how they possess is so much more than that. These inscrutable beings, with ruffled stipes skirting flirtatiously between taxonomic classes, have almost certainly extended my own lifespan; but others are not so lucky.

A guardian angel for one is a destroying angel for another. From 2010 to 2017, over 10,000 people in France were poisoned by mushrooms, with 22 fatal intoxications. In the US from 2010 to 2016, there were 17 mushroom fatalities. These numbers are minute when compared to other poison control center data, such as the 1,000 to 2,000 who die annually from pharmaceutical poisoning, which in 2019 accounted for over 80 percent of all fatal intoxications. However, as Dan Hauser, Dean of Religious Studies, can attest, death by mushroom is a horrific way to go, taking days or even weeks following ingestion. Death caps, responsible for the majority of fatal mycotoxin poisonings worldwide, can cause seizures, liver and kidney failure, intracranial bleeding, coma, and cardiac arrest. By contrast, hallucinogenic mushroom fatalities occur quickly after ingestion, most often when victims drown on their own vomit. This is why the dried caps and stems of fly agaric still sit inside a blue Mason jar on my desk, as who knows when my luck might run out.

Humans of course are not the only organisms who fall dead to mushrooms, who can kill using the most extravagant methods. Some fungi make medieval torture chambers look like daycares, perhaps best illustrated with the case of the Brazilian zombie ant fungus. Spores enter an insect's body and gradually take over its being, using it like a marionette, controlled not from above but within. When the time is right, the mycelium produces sporocarps that erupt from the insect's dying body, suspended from a leaf, which then rains spores down onto the ant trail below. And the cycle begins anew. As insidious and brutal as are its tactics, the fungus also displays a remarkable sophistication. Its methods are not unlike a deterministic god who uses its creation— tricking individuals into the farce of free will—to bring its cosmic master plan to fruition. In this way, the inscrutable fruiting body invites a strange myco-theology, or mushroom metaphysics, of reverence and revulsion—of Mysteries in the truest sense of μυστήρια.

Scala Naturæ

You cannot close your eyes and read this, but try relaxing your eyelids into a feathered squint just so. When you get to the Latin parts, don't skip them. Read, and walk, slowly. Now, imagine that you are in a forest. You are small amidst the trees that surround you. Take a deep breath. The air is cool and wet going in and out of your lungs. You walk between pines, oaks, and beeches, whose branches hold the moisture close to the soil. On the ground, there is leaf litter, pine needles, acorns, and the black droppings of deer and foxes. Your footfall echoes the softness of the earth, and each step is deliberate. Gazing down, you notice beneath the brown of an old oak leaf a burst of scarlet. You bend to the ground and see first one, then four—no, five—mushrooms. This is the one known as fly agaric, with its red and white-speckled pileus that is used in an elixir to kill flies (*Amanita muscaria*). To the left you spot a ringlet of tiny toadstools, so purple they might be some fragile form of amethyst (*Laccaria amethystina*). It is only then that you see, pushing up between two fallen branches, a dozen amber flames that dot the earth. They are emergent chanterelles, gold like dust fallen from the sun (*Cantharellus cibarius*). These beings were not here yesterday, and by tomorrow they may be gone. In contemplating the Here and Now, you are reminded that the forest safeguards secrets and mysteries, and you are humbled to be among them.

Humans have experienced this feeling of awe for the minute and profound for thousands of years. Early Neolithic cave paintings in Spain, at Selva Pascuala, depict a row of thirteen toadstools, and in Algeria, at Tassili n'Ajjer, an adorned figure holds a mushroom bouquet in each hand. The picture becomes clearer once written languages became commonplace. Two thousand years ago, in Classical Antiquity, mushroom reverence was at the heart of religious experience, especially for followers of Mithras, to which early Christianity had close ties.[2] Initiates to the Mysteries of Bacchus, Demeter and Persephone, Isis, Mithras, and Christ ritually consumed psychotropic mushrooms and the fungus

---

[2]Ruck, Carl A. P., Mark A. Hoffman, and Jose Alfredo González Celdrán, *Mushrooms, Myth & Mithras: The Drug Cult that Civilized Europe* (San Francisco: City Lights Books, 2011).

ergot, as well as yeast-fermented beverages like the wine of the Eucharist. Ethnobotanists and religious scholars refer to these substances as entheogens to honor their capacity to inspire visions of God, or to initiate the feeling of divinity in close proximity, if not inside one's own body.

And speaking of initiation, how close Mithraism came to being the dominant religion of Rome! Had it only permitted women initiates, as did Christianity. But in response to the competition, once legalized in the Roman empire, Christian authorities spanning Eurasia and North Africa wasted little time in suppressing not only women in leadership roles, but also other Mystery religions and Christianity's own likeness to them. Despite Late Antique Christianity's intolerance of other faiths, some elements of the Mithraic mushroom cult may have endured, even in the Christian heartland of Europe. If so, they went underground, remaining quiet, almost dormant, for a very long time.

A thousand years later, in the Late Middle Ages, something started to change for us. When I say us, I mean those with European ancestry but also those without. What changed in Europe would affect just about everyone on our entangled planet, mushrooms included. To understand this mysterious and paradoxical change requires first understanding something of the role of the Crusades in engendering the Renaissance.

Firstly, the Crusades, with the Reconquista having been the most protracted manifestation thereof, fostered a mindset of othering and paranoia that made brutal missions of exorcism commonplace. Throughout the Late Middle Ages and Early Modern Period, the Inquisition was just one part of a long period of religious purity tests, forced conversions, genocidal raids, and gynocidal executions throughout Europe and its growing number of colonies.

Secondly, the centuries of othering generated the desire to return to a glorious (and mostly imaginary) Greco-Roman past of European mastery and imperial subjugation. The make-Europa-great-again campaigns included large-scale efforts to translate Classical texts of philosophy, mathematics, and science from Arabic into Latin, which were enhanced with new European treatises. The contributions of Arab scholars to the Classical body of knowledge were largely disregarded or appropriated, and Latinization sought to return the texts to some holier state, debased as they had been all those years by discourse in the infidel languages of Hebrew, Persian, and Arabic.

As the Early Modern era set sail, the knowledges of colonized and Indigenous peoples would become amalgamated into this scientific repertoire, while quelling heretical thought remained equally paramount. So along with the rise of the European academy—the one I attended for my doctorate was founded in 1428—we also see the publication of the witch-hunting manual *Malleus Maleficarum* in 1486.

Willful ignorance and higher education seem difficult to reconcile, and the consequences of this unlikely union still reverberate. One such reverberation is the flawed understanding of the nature of our biodiverse planet, and by extension, the types of souls that form or inhabit the different kinds of bodies. Crusades and pilgrimages to the Holy Land made accessible Aristotle's treatise on the soul, *De Anima*, as it is now most commonly known in the West by its 11th century Latin title. The archbishop Alfanus first translated the treatise from Arabic to Latin, but the book had long been influential among translators of other Abrahamic religious traditions too. But even without the luxury of a translation, or even the luxury of literacy, the Aristotelian organization of lifeforms, from least to most ensouled, had been trickling down through the ages into Christian theology.

Ἄνθρωπος—Human
Ζῷον—Animal
Φυτόν—Plant

In Aristotle's schema, only human souls were capable of reason, while "lower" animals were merely capable of sensation, and plants—including fungi—were lowly nutritive souls, feeding and reproducing but fully incapable of either sensation or reason.

Despite its popularity amongst certain intellectuals, Arthur Lovejoy explains that in the Middle Ages, a strict hierarchical division between lifeforms had not yet infiltrated everyday religious experience. The concept of "divine love" or "goodness" was conceived not as an anthropocentric idea of human compassion or the alleviation of human suffering, but as

> the immeasurable and inexhaustible productive energy, the fecundity of an Absolute not conceived as truly possessing emotions similar to man's . . . [but which] consists primarily rather in the creative or generative than in the redemptive or providential office of deity.[3]

Even though its origins were to be found in Platonic idealism, this medieval "superabundance" of divine generation invites an earthy reverence for those nonhuman beings—like mushrooms—who spontaneously abound, immeasurably, inexhaustibly, and mysteriously.

However, the progenerative fundament common to the Medieval religious experience slowly drifted out of the theophilosophical and scientific mainstream. With the Early Modern additions of further Classical and Arab sources to the corpus of European knowledge, and a renewed religious zealotry that retaliated against the animistic ontological flattening of many colonized peoples, the organization of earthlings into a strict hierarchy with humans at the peak became cemented in the European worldview. As Lovejoy summarizes, "It was not in the thirteenth century but in the nineteenth that *homo* [*sic*] *sapiens* bustled about most

---

[3]Lovejoy, Arthur, *The Great Chain of Being* (Cambridge and London: Harvard University Press, 1978 [1936]), 67.

self-importantly and self-complacently in his infinitesimal corner of the cosmic stage."[4]

Already in 18th-century visual culture, organic life was ranked neatly into a *scala naturæ*, or ladder of being, where man placed himself at the pinnacle of an imagined staircase that ascended into the heavens but descended into dark and murky depths of flesh before terminating on the ground floor of inanimate objects. In typical graphical depictions, the man featured on the top step was only surpassed by divine spirits and the Almighty himself. The man, of Teutonic features, suggests an ideal, which women and the darker complected may not achieve by virtue of our inferior natures. In this schema, nature cannot be transcended. Each step, link, or rung is locked, confined to its design as the Almighty intended.

Below the man, we see depictions of mammalian lifeforms like horses and hares, followed by lesser vertebrates: birds, and then reptiles, frogs, and fish. Below them are the invertebrate lobsters and squids, and one step lower you will find the insects and spiders. Below the arthropods and arachnids are the strange marine organisms like starfish and corals, and below them are the plants with their fruits and vegetables. Finally, on the rung between plant life and inanimate objects, you will find at last the mushrooms. In this hierarchy, fungi are only one step above an hourglass, teakettle, bell, and hammer. They are rendered insensate, insentient, sessile, and essentially expendable.

---

[4]Ibid., 143.

$$\frac{\text{God}}{\text{man}}$$

$$\overline{\text{horse cat}}$$

$$\overline{\text{killdeer duck}}$$

$$\overline{\text{snake frog trout eel}}$$

$$\overline{\text{squid lobster crab cuttlefish}}$$

$$\overline{\text{spider fly caterpillar worm mosquito}}$$

$$\overline{\text{starfish seahorse anemone coral clam oyster sponge}}$$

$$\overline{\text{pineapple fern oak vine yam moss orchid spruce grass coconut}}$$

$$\overline{\text{amanita mold mildew yeast earthstar armillaria puffball chytrid penicillium candida}}$$

$$\overline{\text{cup sextant shoehorn flute table necklace book stove window shovel scale staircase chain ladder}}$$

Systematic representations of the ordered planet, from most sacred to most profane—or within nascent capitalism, most disposable—neglect some of the characteristic features of mushrooms, even on a macroscopic level, that would seem to at least place them on the same rung as plants or corals, not beneath them, nearer the brute stuff of inanimate objects. But as Lovejoy reminds us, "the notion of the Chain of Being, with the assumptions on which it rested, was obviously not a generalization derived from experience, nor was it, in truth, easy to reconcile with the known facts of nature."[5] In our own time, recent scientific investigations into microscopic mycorrhizal networks have raised the fungal profile significantly, but even with the scientific knowledge of the Enlightenment, it was well known that the fungus is a complex organism that works in mysterious ways. Also curious is that among hundreds of years of philosophical discussion into the ranking of creation, fungi are so often conspicuously absent—especially true given Aristotle's suggestion that although mushrooms are most likely to be grouped with plants, someone ought to look further into the matter. With these peculiarities in mind, perhaps there may be more to the story than mere negligence or disinterest, or even the irrational clinging to an unscientific idea.

By contrast to the apparent mycophobia of mainstream Early Modern science, alchemists—Hermetic and heretical—

---

[5]Ibid., 183.

may have hailed mushrooms for their capacity for spectacular growth out of decay, like dying and rising gods. Mushrooms, and fungi more broadly, embody the concept of putrefaction before purification, an important part of the *magnum opus* (Great Work), or the alchemical process of creating the philosopher's stone from *prima materia* (raw materials).

Depicting the maxim of "eternal renewal of things in the midst of decay," alchemical manuscripts often feature images of flasks whose bulbous base shoots gracefully upward on a narrow stalk to finish in a jeweled crown. I think these ornate flasks give some credence to the controversial theory that much of alchemy revolved around the fly agaric, which may even have been the philosopher's stone itself.[6] Once this possibility is raised, much of Hermeticism, revealed in esoteric texts and images, can be understood as steps to prepare the elixir of Mysteries by chemically transmuting the mushroom into a drinkable muscimol.

These iconic—and neurotoxic—toadstools burst out of a white, egglike volva to grow upward, and when the cap separates from the stipe, leaving a fringed ring, it stretches into a ruby-red crown with white flecks like diamonds. Seeing them in a forest, radiant amidst the greens and browns of the

---

[6]Heinrich, Clark, *Magic Mushrooms in Religion and Alchemy* (Rochester, VT: Park Street Press), 165-197. Whatever Heinrich's volume lacks in scholarship it achieves in speculation. Read with a critical eye; I disagree with much of the religious analysis offered, but we did arrive at a similar conclusion on the alchemical Mysteries.

undergrowth, is truly breathtaking—as you may recall from your trip through the woods a few paragraphs ago.

In an alchemical context, the visual symbolism of the mycoform flask and its significance for overcoming decay is especially suggestive in a motif found in early 18th-century illustrated manuscripts. In numerous illustrations, the bejeweled flask holds a crimson ouroboros curled inside its base, all of which rests on the abdomen of an overturned horse. Lying on her back, the horse's legs extend upright, front and back on either side of the flask. Flames spark from the upturned hooves. Written across the horse's body are the words: *Hic est signus [philoso]phicus, sulicet, putrefactionis* (This is a philosophical drawing, namely, of putrefaction). In at least one example circa 1700, there is a caption at the top of the page scrawled in Latin: *Pictura continens homini propria et liberali admiratione, non sine oblectatione spectanti, rei affini* ([This] is a painting of the container in which the freedom proper to humankind, in wonder and not without joy, shall be as he gazes upon some relative thing).[7] Even without reading between the lines, the hallucinatory insinuations of the motif's annotation are clear.

Reference to gazing upon wonders recalls other alchemical writings, such as Mary Anne Atwood's *A Suggestive Inquiry*

---

[7]Translated by the author into English from the Latin in Wilson, William Jerome, "Catalogue of Latin and Vernacular Alchemical Manuscripts in the United States and Canada," *Osiris* 6 (1939): 1-836, p. 216. My thanks to Leonardo Moreno-Alvarez for pointing me toward this publication.

into Hermetic Mystery of 1850: "Our Stone comes with light and with light it is generated, and then it brings forth the clouds, and the darkness which is the mother of all things." She goes on to cite a certain *Compendium of Alchemy*, misattributed to the 14th-century Spanish mystic Raymond Lull, but which probably dates to the 17th century: "*Spiritos fugitivos in aore condensatos, in forma monstrorum diversorum et animalium etiam hominum, qui vadunt sicut nubes, modo hinc modo illuc*" (Fugitive spirits condense in air, in diverse monstrous, animal and human forms, who move like clouds hither and thither).[8] She later describes initiation into the Grand Mysteries as akin to death in its

> dreadful aspect; it is all horror trembling, sweating, and affrightment. But this scene once over, a miraculous and divine light displays itself, and shining plains, and flowery meadows, open on all hands before them. Here they are entertained with hymns and dances, and with sublime and sacred knowledges, and with reverend and holy visions.[9]

In another section, she explains that the "descent," or coming down, is not difficult, but the "ascent" is where things can get out of hand, as when one swallows hallucinogenic neurotoxins

---

[8] Atwood, M. A., *A Suggestive Inquiry into Hermetic Mystery* (Glastonbury: The Lost Books, 2016 [1850]), 215.
[9] Ibid., 221.

and proceeds to vomit explosively before being arrested by visions. It is for that reason that "every precaution has been taken to keep the way a secret from the world, as well for its own sake."[10] Keeping "the way" secret keeps the uninitiated and inexperienced out of danger, but so too in this sentiment does the "way" seem delicate, if not vulnerable and in need of protection; we might recall that "mystery" and "mystic'" are derived from the Greek μυείν ("to hide" or "to shut"), from which "mute" is also derived. Secrets must be secreted away, for your sake and for theirs. Atwood continues that the Mysteries, or

> the opposive powers display their mutual forces in discordant dissolute array, as the Alchemists, with all who have been profoundly experienced in this ground, relate such in his own instructive way, warning about the conduct through it, and the many real though chimerical horrors and enticing phantoms that haunt around, guarding the secret chamber of their mineral soul. For as the sage in Enoch declares it, lead and tin are not produced from the earth as the primary fountain of their production; but there is an angel standing upon it, and that angel struggles to prevail.[11]

Fragile on the ground, easily overlooked, the sentineled passageway into the Hermetic Mysteries certainly seems to usher an intense trip for those who dare.

---

[10]Ibid., 205.
[11]Ibid., 214-215.

Visions of devils and beastly spirits push us back to the strange motif of a flask, set atop the stomach of an overturned horse, that brings forth such wondrous forms. About this image, 18th-century monk and mystic Antoine-Joseph Pernety wrote,

> This symbolizes for the regular Chemist warm horse manure, that, through its soft warmth is suitable for digestion and putrefaction; however, the Hermetic Chemists mean the material of their *art in the black* or in putrefaction.[12]

These lines are enigmatic, but the identification of horse manure as an alchemical substance of great importance is highly suggestive.

To explore this idea further, we might turn our attention back to the red-painted ouroboros in the base of the crowned flask. In a 15th-century Greek alchemical poem, the self-consuming serpent is described in cryptic detail:

---

[12]Author's emphasis; translated by the author into English from the Dutch translation in Van Lennep, Jacques, *Alchemie*, 143; cf. fig. 260. Van Lennep quotes Pernety's *Dictionnaire mytho-hermétique, dans lequel on trouve les allégories fabuleuses des poètes, les métaphores, les énigmes et les termes barbares des philosophes hermétiques expliqués* (Réédition: Bibliotheca Hermetica, 1972 [1758]), 516. Another example of the motif is given in Grillot de Givry, Émile, *Illustrated Anthology of Sorcery, Magic and Alchemy*, 358, fig. 333.

A dragon springs therefrom which, when exposed
In horse's excrement for twenty days,
Devours his tail 'til naught thereof remains.
This dragon, whom they Ouroboros ['Tail-biter'] call,
Is white in looks and spotted in his skin.[13]

Besides the red-and-white spotted serpent who might be camouflaged against a field of fly agarics—or, perhaps, may be one of them—the dung heap that grows the dragon is still used today to nurture the buttons, creminis, and portobellos that are later harvested for human consumption. Furthermore, the word "ouroboros" can be translated as "urine-biter," which may "refer to the widely documented practice of filtering and fortifying the entheogenic properties of the mushroom as the urinous metabolite by means of passing it through the human body"; put simply, this passage runs thick with allusions to the alchemical magic of the mushroom.[14]

As is notoriously common among efforts to decipher esoteric and allegorical alchemical manuscripts, interpretations, including this one, are dubious. That said, my interpretation of the motif—that the crowned flask atop an equiform heap of horse's dung represents the attempted cultivation of *A. muscaria*—does lend some additional

---

[13]Quoted in Holmyard, E. J., *Alchemy*, New York: Dover Publications, Inc., 1990 [1957], 159.
[14]Ruck et al., *Mushrooms, Myth & Mithras*, 218.

weight to the claim that alchemical manuscripts displaying mutilated and dismembered human bodies are visual code to reference the harvesting of fly agaric mushrooms, which, like others of their kind, regenerate mysteriously after having been beheaded.[15] In alchemical terms, the homunculus prevails. And in the bizarre world of fungi, which is also our world, spores feed on rotten stipes, and life flourishes from death.

However, not all fungal life regenerates in the same way. Even mushrooms that are not harvested still seem to vanish overnight, and the apparent regeneration is neither immediate nor predictable. In some cases, like the earthstars of the *Astraeus* genus, they tend to wither, like demons cast from heaven, into astral shells; or, like the inky caps of the *Coprinus* genus, they are overcome with their own juices before seeping, black and wet, back into the soil. In other cases, from one day to the next, they seem to just disappear into the dark earth or ether. But when mushrooms vanish from plain sight, who—or what—vanishes them?

Likewise, when they inexplicably erupt from the ground, ribald and ripe, what—or who—prompts them? Even Francis Bacon, who dabbled in alchemy, wondered in *Sylva Sylvarum* (1670) at the mushroom's "strange" ability to grow "up so hastily, as in a night."[16] There must be some underground

---

[15]Heinrich, *Magic Mushrooms in Religion and Alchemy*, 180-181.
[16]Bacon, Francis, *Sylva Sylvarum*, Century VI.546.

foreplay at work to erect those strange fruits with their explosion of spores. Perhaps the chaste, Early Modern mind recognized those sexual thrustings from the earth, so often phallic shaped and positioned in a circle as if gathering around some magic womb or vagina, and knew that these organisms cannot have been fashioned by the Heavenly Father, the virginal Christ, but rather some other spirit—"the evil ferment of the earth," perhaps.[17] As Percy Bysshe Shelley wrote in 1820,

> And agarics, and fungi, with mildew and mould
> Started like mist from the wet ground cold;
> Pale, fleshy, as if the decaying dead
> With a spirit of growth had been animated![18]

Francis Bacon associated mushrooms with the incubus, and posited that they grow on dead and rotting trees the way hair and fingernails keep growing on a corpse.[19] Peter Breughel the Elder depicted a living hell, with mushrooms sprouting as diadems from a demon's crown, as wicked hordes are driven

---

[17]Nicander, *Alexipharmaca*, 521, quoted and translated in Rev. William Houghton, "Notices of Fungi in Greek and Latin Authors," *The Annals and Magazine of Natural History, Including Zoology, Botany and Geology*, Vol. XV, edited by Albert C. L. G. Günther, William S. Dallas, William Caruthers, and William Francis, 22-49 (London: Taylor & Francis, 1985), 23-24.
[18]Shelley, Percy Bysshe, *The Sensitive Plant*, 1820.
[19]Bacon, *Sylva Sylvarum*, Century VI.552.

into the toothy maw of eternal damnation.[20] Once known as Judas' ear, the common name of *Auricularia auricula-judae* has been shortened to Jew's ear, the antisemitic epithet recalling the connection between apostasies of Jewry and Witchery, evident in Hans Baldung Grien's 1508 woodcut *The Witches*. There, naked hags in chiaroscuro rove around a great emanating urn with a Hebraic inscription. Other circles drawn on the ground in fruiting fungal bodies are called *hexenkringen*, *Hexenringe*, and *ronds des sorcières* in Dutch, German, and French respectively, each of which means "witch rings," the unholy circumferences of midnight revelries with the devil. Rings of mushrooms were known in the English-speaking world too as places demarcating "the Rendezvous of Witches."[21] And as for those mushroom varieties whose bioluminescence eerily lights up woods and wetlands, these organisms can only be the work of Lucifer himself, whose name means "bringing light."

In what he calls "anti-vegetal ethics," Michael Marder observes how Christian theology played a part in banishing plants from the realm of the good, possibly due to the roles of trees and fruit in the *lapsus humani* on that fateful day in the Garden of Eden, and of a particularly complicit tree in the

---

[20]Breughel the Elder, Peter, *The Last Judgement*, 1558. Engraving, Metropolitan Museum of Art, New York City.
[21]For example, see: More, Henry, *A Collection of Several Philosophical Writings of Dr. Henry More* (London: James Flesher for William Morden Book-Seller in Cambridge, 1662), 121.

crucifixion of Christ.[22] This ethics against greenery seems to run counter to the medieval conception of goodness and love as parallel to fecundity and the *horror vacui* of "nature." And yet, it took root. To reiterate from above, since the Greeks, vegetation had not been considered of great intellectual or moral depth. Aristotle had long since identified plants, a category that tenuously included fungi, as the least ensouled of the three varieties of life.

Following his line of thought, Pseudo-Aristotle too reasoned a plant as "an incomplete thing"; centuries later, Francis Bacon identified mushrooms as "imperfect plants," rendering these organisms doubly defective.[23] But in the comparatively complex Linnaean context of the later Early Modern era and the Enlightenment, it is likely that colonization played a large part in rendering plants and their kin as not just imperfect or soulless but akin to wickedness.

With the theory of environmental determinism looming over so many Early Modern colonial endeavors, the question of vegetal—and others who pass as such—denigration may not be shrouded in much mystery after all. In 1750, the influential French philosopher Montesquieu conjured the idea that climate determines human behavior and cultural

---

[22]Marder, Michael, *The Philosopher's Plant* (New York: Columbia University Press, 2014), 68-73.

[23]On Pseudo-Aristotle, see: Marder, Michael, *Plant-Thinking: A Philosophy of Vegetal Life* (New York City: Columbia University Press, 2013), 23. On Francis Bacon, see: *Sylva Sylvarum*, Century VI.546.

characteristics. He reasoned, "If we draw near the south, we fancy ourselves removed from all morality; the strongest passions multiply all manner of crimes," and yet, somehow, at the same time, "The heat of the climate may be so excessive as to deprive the body of all vigor and strength."[24] It is as if the hyperbolic growth of tropical plants sucks all the vigor and courage from the air, leaving humans with nothing but "indolence"—or at least with only enough vigor left for licentious and other immoral acts.

In numerous British colonial accounts, for example, of the jungles of Southeast Asia, plants are thought to have contributed to the moral demise of the human populations there.[25] To the British mind, having to work for one's food, rather than merely reaching up and plucking it from some green tree, was part of what it means to be a fully developed human being. By enabling sloth, lush vegetation and its sweet fruits greedily prevented these equatorial peoples from moral, cultural, and even biological maturation.

Perhaps something similar happened with mushrooms, but unlike the phytophobia of exotic colonized lands, mycophobia developed within the European homeland. Although they graced the dinner tables of nobleman

---

[24]Montesquieu, *The Spirit of Laws*, translated by Thomas Nugent (Berkeley and Los Angeles: University of California Press, 1977 [1750]), Book XIV, Chapter 2, 12-13, 247.

[25]Tiffin, Sarah, *Southeast Asia in Ruins: Art and Empire in the Early 19th Century* (Singapore: National University of Singapore Press, 2017).

and farmer alike, foraging for mushrooms was primarily the purview of the peasant. The lowly peasant, whose base instincts keep her "closer to nature," could be seen rummaging through meadows and forests, lazily plucking weird fruits from the earth rather than tending crops and cultivating higher manners and morals. Consider Ernest Bloch's 1912 photograph taken in Satigny, Switzerland, of a toothless old woman dressed in black like a fairy tale witch, holding a massive mushroom in each hand. A foraging companion of mine in Flanders recalled memories of her childhood in Poland learning the different wild edibles from her grandmother. The Slavic word *baba*, meaning grandmother, midwife, and witch, is closely associated with mushrooms, including edibles like boletes (*babka*, which also means little witch, little granny).[26] But a matrilineal knowledge is so often a taboo knowledge.

Increasingly associated with the immorals of poverty, female sexuality, witchery, and otherworldly hallucinations, by the time of the Enlightenment, mushrooms had been relegated to the bottom of the *scala naturæ*, opposite the pallid man at the pinnacle, who lords over the others while boasting

---

[26]Dugan, Frank Matthews, *Fungi in the Ancient World* (St. Paul, MN: American Phytopathological Society, 2008), 91. I have recently acquired a vintage postcard from Russia that features the hut of Baba Yaga, the witch of Slavic folklore. Her wooden hut stands on chicken legs in an eerie wood with bats flying overhead, snakes crawling over rotten stumps, and a variety of mushrooms sprouting up in the foreground.

of divine proximity.[27] Perhaps it was fear and revulsion of the erotic explosions from the earth, the seduction of delicious edibles next to deadly lookalikes, secret female knowledge of which is which, or the deceptive vaultings of the mind into some other realm, that unjustly cast mushrooms so far down the hierarchy of existence, deep into heretical realms. But as the alchemists and peasants knew, fungi prosper on the downtrodden. They know how to take abuse and transmute it into gold.

[27]Dugan, Frank M., "Fungi, Folkways & Fairy Tales: Mushrooms & Mildews in Stories, Remedies & Rituals, from Oberon to the Internet," *North American Fungi* 3.7 (2008): 23-72; Adrian Morgan, *Toads and Toadstools: The Natural History, Mythology and Cultural Oddities of this Association* (Berkeley: Celestial Arts Publishing, 1995).

FALL

Shaggy mane
Dutch: *inktzwam* (ink mushroom)
French: *coprin chevelu* (hairy coprine)
Latin: *Coprinus comatus*

Shaggy manes are gilled mushrooms and the most easily identifiable of the genus *Coprinus*. They have a grey or white bell-shaped cap with soft scruffs that tuft out from its surface. When young, the bottom of the cap is still attached to the stipe, and those are the best for gathering. As they grow older and the cap separates from the stipe to form the bell, the ink for which the *Coprinus* members are famous turns the cap black until it melts gradually back into the earth.

This species in particular is delicious and edible even raw, but to be on the safe side, wild mushrooms should always be cooked before eating. An additional precaution is in order with this mushroom in that others of its genus contain the toxin coprine, which inhibits the enzyme that processes alcohol. So while some others of the genus are also edible, they should not be consumed with alcoholic beverages. Imbibing with a side of gently sauteed shaggy manes is perfectly safe, but one should take precautions in all cases to positively identify foraged mushrooms before consuming them, and to know all the related risks.

Harvested shaggy manes should be eaten immediately, or they will disintegrate into an inky black liquid. They can be cooked and refrigerated for a couple days, but they cannot be preserved through the usual means of freezing or drying.

However, if you do mistakenly end up with a batch of black, liquified toadstools, you can strain out the remaining solids and use the ink for dying fabrics or paper or for writing and drawing, similar to sumi.

Note: A similar mushroom, Old Man of the Woods (*Strobilomyces floccopus*), is in the family of boletes (*Boletaceae*) but shares some visual characteristics with the shaggy mane in that they are both grey in color and scruffy looking, and both have white flesh that is delicious when cooked. In my experience, shaggy manes are more often found in meadows, and Old Men tend to take to the woods. To tell them apart, look at the underside of the cap. If it has a sponge-like surface rather than gills, it's probably an Old Man of the Woods. Like other boletes, the Old Man can be dried to preserve for later use.

PART II

METAPHOR

Bawdy Parts

Have you ever considered, when eating a mushroom, that you are eating the sex organ of the fungus? Those who eat dandelions and nasturtiums are familiar with this pornographic revelation since flowers are the angiosperm's . . . well, just ask Georgia O'Keefe. A mushroom is something like a penis that ejaculates millions of sperm cells—spores, in this case—that drift through the air and fall softly on the endometrium that is the earth. There, embedded in moist, woody soil, they meet compatible spores and germinate, reproducing the fungal life cycle. How appropriate that in Ojibwe, the word for mushrooms (*puhpowee*) is also a mystical idiom describing the spiritual force that raises them from the earth overnight; at the same time, it refers to "other shafts that rise mysteriously in the night."[1]

Metaphorically, mushrooms are apt and widespread symbols of explosive fecundity. In English, mushroom is a noun and to mushroom is a verb used to communicate rapid spread or growth—like those mysterious nighttime shafts, things "pop up like mushrooms" and "mushroom into" something bigger. In her 1959 poem "Mushrooms," Sylvia Plath makes clever use of grammatical ambiguity to relay a mounting conquest, of sorts. Her poem's fungal genitalia wield their silent, emergent power:

Soft fists insist on
Heaving the needles
The leafy bedding,

Even the paving.
Our hammers, our rams,
Earless and eyeless,

Perfectly voiceless,
Widen the crannies,
Shoulder through the holes.

[1]Kimmerer, Robin Wall, "Learning the Grammar of Animacy," *Anthropology of Consciousness* 28.2 (2017): 128-134, 131.

Mushrooms mushrooming, they rejoice in their numbers: "So many of us! So many of us!" They constitute a persistent insurrection, unassuming yet overwhelming, as they meekly assume their inheritance:

Nudgers and shovers
In spite of ourselves.
Our kind multiplies:

We shall by morning
Inherit the earth.
Our foot's in the door.[2]

There is an ominous aura creeping out from the poem's last lines cast by the bodiless bodies cracking through Earth's cellar door not only by sheer force of will and strength of numbers, but by some strategy or prophecy known only to their kind. Surrender to your fate, lie back—resistance is futile and fungal. This beautiful nightmare is an erotic apocalypse of the living dead; these earthborn masters rising up from shallow graves are indifferent to treaties, allies, conditions, or consent.

At the time Sylvia (whose name means "from the forest") wrote this poem, she confessed that she was learning to be true

---

[2]Plath, Sylvia, *The Collected Poems*, edited by Ted Hughes (New York: Harper Perennial, 1992), 139-140.

to her own "weirdnesses." And at this time, in a New England November inundated with fall leaves and fungal bounties, she almost certainly knew she was pregnant with her first child.

> Overnight, very
> Whitely, discreetly,
> Very quietly . . .

Within three years, she would gas her brilliant mind to death, overwhelmed as it was by the slow, persistent pressures of motherhood, wifedom, and a world that seems fated for men. These are the kind that crack sidewalks and fissure cerebella.

Part of the patriarchal legacy that Sylvia fought against during her abbreviated life included what Mary Daly calls the gynocidal agendas of Early Modern Christendom.[3] The connections of witchery and mushrooms were not limited to foraging habits and alleged potions of the accused but rather extends, if you will, into the metaphorical mushroom of male sexuality. The *Malleus Maleficarum* describes numerous accounts of witches having robbed men of their "virile member" or, if not vanished entirely, bewitched it with impotent flaccidity or any of various erectile dysfunctions.[4]

---

[3]Daly, Mary, *Gyn/Ecology: The Metaethics of Radical Feminism* (Boston: Beacon Press, 1990 [1978]).
[4]Kramer, Heinrich and James Spencer, *Malleus Maleficarum*, translated by Reverend Montague Summers (New York: Dover Publications, Inc., 1971 [1928]).

One witch allegedly had a collection of penises secreted away in a bird's nest (the largest belonged to the parish priest). Witches might also criminally refuse a man's advances, even those of her own husband. This absurd degree of denial, misogyny, and castration anxiety dealt a pyromaniac's death blow to many innocent women, but as Mary maintains, The Burning Times continue even now. I suspect Sylvia would agree.

* * *

In Linnaean taxonomy, the species name of the discreet, persistent mushroom might be *pudicus*, Latin for pure, chaste, or modest. Alas, that mushroom does not, as yet, exist. Instead, we have the *Phallus impudicus*, the immodest, the shameless, the obscene penis, whose conical tip flares from a long, slender stipe. When young, they burst forth from testicular eggs, some of whom are harvested in Northern Europe where they are known as a potent aphrodisiac. While its impudent shape oozes fertility, sexuality, and love, its aroma harkens death, with an odor of carrion that attracts flies to its sticky, gelatinous tip, that nearly drips with spores, who are carried afield on winged and grotesquely bristled legs. This fungal member's ambivalent nature is well described by its colloquial name, "stinkhorn." Death's putrid stench on the doorstep, invited by a suggestive Valentine.

Advancing the necrophiliac's false premise of love, the mushroom cloud delivers on the necropolitician's promise of death. Neither cloud nor mushroom, the idiomatic epithet epitomizes the image of nuclear warfare. Hiroshima, Nagasaki, Bikini Atoll, Alamogordo—beginning with a minuscule split atom that produces an immediate chain reaction, the blast wave of nuclear detonation rapidly ascends, the mushroom's stem like the updraft of a miles-high chimney. A vortex ring skirts the shaft, resembling the stipe ring of a parasol mushroom. Rising ever higher into the atmosphere, the ascending gases begin to stabilize, at which point they cease their ascension and begin dispersing outward from the stem into a broad pileus. But this mushroom cap is full of radioactive particles and fission detritus, which, as the gases reach equilibrium, begin drifting down, like spores, as deadly fallout. Adrian Morgan points to a possible etymology of "toadstool" stemming from the German word for death, *Todt*.[5] As Robert Oppenheimer saw what he had done, he quoted Lord Krishna: "Now I am become death, destroyer of worlds."

Oppenheimer's Manhattan Project had developed two types of atom bomb, lovingly referred to as Fat Man and Little Boy. The Fat Man, with his fissioned plutonium (^{239}Pl), was dropped on Nagasaki, and the Little Boy, with his fissioned enriched uranium (^{235}U), was dropped on Hiroshima. Together, their nocturnal emissions killed, maimed, or mutated hundreds of thousands of people. Some mushrooms, even metaphorical ones, are deadly poisonous.

---

[5] Morgan, *Toads and Toadstools*, 19.

Like Kin

Unwittingly mycophilic, 1950s slang would have it that there's a fungus among us and a penis between us. Affiliates of promiscuity, fertility, and inexplicable growth, the imaginings of mushrooms—fecund or fœtid, lewd or lurid—dramatically deviate from those of the organism of which a mushroom is but one bawdy part. The word "fungus" bears the connotation of parasitic growth, of leeching, or colonizing at the expense of other lives. Imagine a forest floor speckled with rotten mushrooms, each powdered with sticky grey mold. In this dark wood, deviant fungi prey on their fellows in a viscous cannibal orgy.

The invasive white-nose syndrome fungus (*Pseudogymnoascus destructans*) has suffocated and starved millions of North American bats, rendering some species regionally extinct. Another invasive species, the amphibian chytrid fungus (*Batrachochytrium dendrobatidis*), infects frogs' skin cells so that their skin peels off layer by layer, a horrible death that has already claimed over 100 amphibian species. Declinations and extinctions are found globally, and like bats, the loss of frogs can derail entire ecosystems. As for humans, spores that infect our feet and sex organs, ringworm brands on hands, molds that rot the lungs in our chests—all are mycoses that infect some billion of us a year. Recall the sitcom trope of the date night during which anti-fungal cream is unearthed in a medicine cabinet and a taxi is promptly hailed. A fungus is a deal-breaker.

The funk of rot that spreads through thin air to invade damp, private places recalls a childhood memory from the trailer house where I was raised, nestled in the wooded Chippewa Hills. My parents awoke one morning, outraged to find tiny brown mushrooms sprouting up from the aged green carpet in a corner of their bedroom, a sure sign of rotten wood beneath them. To me, it seemed as magical as if they'd found ground-nesting birds living under the bed, but I now sympathize with their reaction. My house too has seen its share of mushy floors. When I bought it, the subfloors and joists had succumbed to the dry rot fungus *Serpula lacrymans* (which should have been a deal-breaker), so they all had to be ripped out and replaced. A few months later, dozens of houses in my neighborhood were demolished because of mold infestations that erupted during weeks-long flooding in the aftermath of Hurricane Florence. Even in my archaeological dealings with ship timbers, wood-degrading aquatic fungi help whittle entire galleons down to a few soggy splinters. And yet, despite these architectural myco-aggressions, I can still hear the old alchemist whispering in Latin: *putrefactionis ante purificationem.*

To a lesser degree, plants are also agents of architectural destruction. Vines suctioning onto siding, roots cracking foundations, and trees splitting the stone masonry of historic ruins all contribute to the never-ending task of "vegetation management" when it comes to architectural conservation. As Caitlin DeSilvey notes, concepts of restoration and preservation "privilege recovery of an imagined original state over the discovery of possible future states."[6] How un-alchemical this attitude of recovery is!

For a species so enamored with building, it is difficult to appreciate decay. We build houses and ships and monuments only to spend eternity trying to maintain their structural integrity against the entropic forces tearing them down. There are active agents in the world, fungal and botanical agents, who do everything in their power to destroy what we construct. But we shouldn't hold it against them. Why not? Because their destructive energies, spent liquifying timbers and pulverizing stone monuments, make possible the new. It is only through such putrefaction that proliferation, with its embedded emphasis on *life*, might occur. We tend to think that death preys on life, stalks it in dark cloaks, but life preys on death too. Because life feeds on life, life needs life to *life*.

* * *

Like the word "mushroom," "plant" is also both noun and verb. To plant is to seed, to root, to cultivate, to find a spot and stay there. To mushroom, by contrast, is to abound, to effluviate. For organisms that have long been seen as variations of the same, linguistically, they are opposites. Nonetheless, there

---

[6]Caitlin DeSilvey, "A Positive Passivity: Entropy and Ecology in the Ruins," 285-305 in *Heritage Ecologies*, eds. Torgeir Rinke Bangstad and Þóra Pétursdóttir (London and New York: Routledge 2021), 304.

is compatibility. As part plant, part fungus, perhaps it's not surprising that "lichen" also shares this trait of being noun and verb.[7] Although it looks the part of mere plant, a lichen is an inscrutable nested organism composed of both kingdoms. In a strange partnership, the cooperative of the lichen consists of one part fungus, called a mycobiont, and one part alga, or photobiont. Algal parts photosynthesize for the fungus, who anchors and protects the algae while metabolizing other nutrients from air, wood, and stone for the shared pantry of this composite organism, or holobiont. Yet, still others, including fungi like yeasts along with various bacteria, also join this holobiontic arrangement—that is, they lichenize. To lichenize is to soften categories, appeal to opposites, allow for permeation and permutation. To lichen is to seek kin that look not like you. Various fungi, algae, and bacteria conjoin to become, like kin, lichen.

It is tempting to anthropomorphize such complementary interobject relations. Merlin Sheldrake insists on the promiscuity of fungi, adhering as they do to so few taxonomical restraints.[8] Compared to human social norms, they seem relatively uninhibited, if not indiscriminate in their extra-fungal relations. Alternatively, lichens might lead us to think of polyamorous relationships. Pushing this ontologically foreign being into familiar human constructs is

---

[7]Sheldrake, Merlin, *Entangled Life: How Fungi Make Our Worlds, Change Our Minds, and Shape Our Futures* (New York: Random House, 2020), 86, 88.
[8]Ibid.

nothing new; nineteenth-century researchers first conceived of mycobiont and photobiont as a master-slave relation. This analogy postulated a false equivalence that stunted further inquiry for decades, yet we keep making the same mistake by anthropomorphizing lichen constituents to teach us lessons about queer sexuality or the merits of polygamy.

If there is a lesson for lichens to teach us, it may be that natural partnerships are not necessarily sexual by nature. This lesson would suggest—if Jane Bennett and Ian Bogost are correct and some kind of anthropomorphosis is the only way to reveal the complexity of extrahuman ontologies—that we might better liken lichens to the symbiosis of multispecies households.[9] Lichens, in their asexual, multi-kingdom expansion, are similar to when dog-human-fish-bee-lizard combines with bolete-polypore-devil's horn-russula and oak-moss-clover-sage-lily-jasmine, to exchange with each other in ways that are aesthetic, emotional, nutritional, and territorial, thereby fashioning the multispecies unit of a home.

There is a way that anthropomorphic metaphor can lead to interspecies isomorphic revelation, but it first requires careful and deliberate shapeshifting into equilibrium with the anthropomorphized. Such eerie transposition allows us to wonder more completely at the ontology, agency, and

---

[9]Bennett, Jane, *Vibrant Matter* (Durham: Duke University Press, 2010), 99; Bogost, Ian, *Alien Phenomenology: Or, What It's Like to Be a Thing* (Minneapolis: University of Minnesota Press 2012), 65-66; Harman, Graham, *Object-Oriented Ontology* (London: Penguin UK, 2018), 86-88.

organization of extrahuman entities, rather than merely to project our own proclivities onto them.

And if this metaphorical bodysnatching can be achieved, we might experience an anthropomorphism that is oddly de-anthropocentric. As Kimmerer explains, Algonquian languages make it possible for just about any lively thing—not just mushrooms, plants, and lichens—to be a verb: in other words, for a person (or a mole, a stone, or a leaf) "to be a hill" or "to be a bay." In this way, the human speaker might move herself into the animated, living realm of the hill or the bay:

> A bay is a noun only if water is *dead*. When *bay* is a noun, it is defined by humans, trapped between its shores and contained by the word. But the verb *wiikegama*—to be a bay—releases the water from bondage and lets it live. "To *be* a bay" holds the wonder that, for this moment, the living water has decided to shelter itself between these shores, conversing with cedar roots and a flock of baby mergansers. Because it could do otherwise—become a stream or an ocean or a waterfall, and there are verbs for that, too. To be a hill, to be a sandy beach, to be a Saturday, all are possible verbs in a world where everything is alive. Water, land, and even a day, the language a mirror for seeing the animacy of the world, the life that pulses through all things, through pines and nuthatches and mushrooms.[10]

---

[10]Kimmerer, "Learning the Language of Animacy," 2017, 131; cf. *Braiding Sweetgrass*, 55.

Reasoning with Indigenous languages helps us all understand that just as we *anthropomorphize*, mushrooms *mycophorize* and lichens *lichenophorize*. Importantly, to be like lichen is more than just likening them to us. It entails getting close enough to let the awe of difference in. Before a fungus and an alga can lichenize, they must somehow recognize their differences as well as their compatibilities. In their language, the fungus has to *be* the alga, and the alga the fungus. This is how we lichen, how we seek kin that look not like us. Although none can fully grasp the alien other, symbionts use some kind of isomorphic metaphor to reach closer and seek ontological compatibility.

As we learn the lessons of lichens, we are (re)learning that so many extrahuman kin experience cooperation, competition, and collaboration far beyond our wildest personifying fantasies. At a time when the excesses of globalization have made existence dangerous for so many of us bionts, when humans are reasonably beseeched to "make kin not babies," we might also unlearn seeing the forest for the trees, whose verticality makes them so easy to anthropomorphize; instead, let's get low, refocus our eyes, and see the forest for the fungus.[11]

---

[11]Haraway, Donna, *Staying with the Trouble: Making Kin in the Chthulucene* (Durham: Duke University Press, 2016), 102-103 and n. 18.

WINTER

Fly agaric
Dutch: *vliegenzwam* (fly mushroom)
French: *fausse oronge* (false Caesar's mushroom) or
amanite tue-mouches (fly-killing amanita)
Latin: *Amanita muscaria*

This mushroom is widespread across the Northern Hemisphere, and lately, I've noticed many individuals appearing in the South Carolina lowlands in the wet dead of winter. As are many of their fellows, fly agarics are outstandingly beautiful, with white-freckled caps that may be apple-red, lemon-yellow, or the color of ripe nectarines. A graceful ring flounces around the stipe, which grows from a soft, white egg. They are also iconic across many cultures for their association with fairy tales and because they have been a focal point in religious practices for thousands of years. The fly agaric's magic and mystery stem from its hallucinogenic properties, caused by the toxin muscimol, from which its Latin name is derived. This toxin has also inspired the toadstool's names in other languages, which refer to its ability to bait and kill houseflies.

Field guides will tell you not to eat it or any other of the genus *Amanita*, and with good reason. Almost all of them are poisonous. Poisonous and beautiful.

And for these reasons, I'm also going to advise against another bad habit that people have started, which is making mushroom bouquets.

First of all, pluck a poisonous mushroom, and you're likely to get toxins all over your hands, which will contaminate everything else, including the edibles, that you touch. Due to an unusually rainy New England in the summer of 2021, mushrooms have become bountiful, and so have new foragers. Not surprisingly, dozens of mushroom poisonings were reported in the month of July alone.

Second of all, picking mushrooms for a bouquet robs the fungus of its ability to reproduce. It's a forced hysterectomy, a brutal castration, for no reason other than to have something pretty on a dining room table for a day—or, depending on the mushroom, an hour. Without earth and water to feed them, even the lovely and graceful fly agaric will shrivel into an unrecognizable, colorless stick.

And without reproduction, the mycorrhizal fungus will be unable to continue supporting the forests of birch, pine, larch, and spruce with whom it engages in a symbiotic relationship.

If you're not going to eat it, leave it alone. Instead, take a photo and post it to the citizen science app iNaturalist so that you might help scientists track changes to fungal populations through the seasons as Earth's climate warms. After all, even in the heat of the Deep South, there's nothing normal about ringing in the New Year next to a spot of red emerging from dead pine needles.

PART III

MYCOLOGY

Merry Men

Although humans have only emerged on the other side of one extinction event so far, at the Terminal Pleistocene some 12,000 years ago, other earthlings are seasoned veterans of obliteration. The moment before Earth's fifth mass extinction, a meteor struck Chicxulub, Mexico, likely forming a vast mushroom cloud. That cloud of debris is famous for killing the dinosaurs some 66 million years ago. Yet other life went on, and due to fossilized spores, paleontologists now understand that it was fungi who expanded and facilitated the regrowth of forests, starting with ferns and gymnosperms, and eventually angiosperms. Out of these fungal-laden forests came the mammals like us who thrive among them.

Fungi had prior experience jump-starting terrestrial ecosystems after a catastrophic extinction. Known as the Great Dying, the Permian-Triassic extinction 262 million years ago eliminated over 90 percent of floral and faunal species. Despite the grisly statistics, Earth's biomass recuperated following a fungal spike that facilitated the eventual repopulation of plants and animals, including those ill-fated dinosaurs and the mammals who would supersede them.

Now that a mass extinction of our own design is underway, mushrooms may again play a vital role in the survival of Earth's plants and other critters. That said, there is a certain irony to how much of the current extinction event is due to human exploitation of 300-million-year-old substances that only formed because fungi could not keep up with the decay.[1] According to the evolutionary lag theory, fungi enabling the global expansion of tropical coal forests had not yet diversified sufficiently to cope with their demise as the climate suddenly cooled. The Carboniferous Rainforest Collapse heaped up dead plant bodies that, left undecomposed, morphed over millions of years into today's fossil fuels.

Fungi seem to have learned from their error and have been working hard at decomposition ever since. Knowing how much of human life, prehistoric and modern, is dependent on fungal activities, it is all the more perplexing that these

---

[1] It should be noted that this long-held geological theory has recently been challenged; see: Nelson et al., "Delayed Fungal Evolution Did Not Cause the Paleozoic Peak in Coal Production," *PNAS* 113.9 (2016): 2442-2447.

organisms have been relegated so far down the chain of being. Arthur Lovejoy noted how paradoxical it is that hierarchies of being became so entrenched at around the same time as the geocentric model of the universe went extinct, which was also around the same time as the first harvesting of coal forests to fuel industrialism. One might expect a certain humility to result from knowing how insignificant one's planet is, and how small we are on it; and yet, the Early Modern mindset embraced a nonsensical theophilosophical justification to ensure human flourishing above all others, at all costs. Ernest Becker mused that this response was only natural in the face of such humbling scientific revelations because man is "a trembling animal who pulls the world down around his shoulders as he clutches for protection and support and tries to affirm in a cowardly way his feeble powers."[2] Coal burning, farms polluting, loggers razing, and yet Lovejoy could somehow offer an optimistic forecast:

[C]ertain consequences which might naturally have resulted from the introduction of the new spatio-temporal scale and scheme of things actually manifested themselves tardily and partially, though, as we have seen, with some fluctuation, and that their full repercussion is perhaps still in the future.[3]

---

[2]Becker, Ernest, *The Denial of Death* (New York: Free Press, 1973), 139.
[3]Lovejoy, *Great Chain of Being*, 143.

Decades later, amidst a climate crisis that not even he could foresee, Lovejoy's optimism resonates with current scholarship that insists on de-anthropocentrism and the crucial role of fungi in regulating and rebalancing Earth's systems.

Anna Tsing's anthropological research into matsutake forests in Japan and the American Pacific Northwest has offered a cautiously hopeful perspective on how mushrooms may provide a way out of Anthropocene ruination.[4] With admirable nuance, she considers the foragers, loggers, corporations, and protestors contributing to forest dynamics, but she really spotlights the nonhuman actors. She proposes that by understanding the complexities of matsutake in eco- and economic systems, we might better appreciate the deeply embedded powers of nonhuman entities. Mushrooms have healed Japanese soil, air, and water after nuclear bombs irradiated Hiroshima and Nagasaki.[5] They absorbed toxic radiocesium from nuclear testing during the Cold War, and they're doing it again in the aftermath of the Fukushima disaster.[6] With time, they can heal the decades of old-growth forest annihilation in the Pacific Northwest too.

---

[4]Tsing, Anna, *The Mushroom at the End of the World: On the Possibility of the Life in Capitalist Ruins* (Minneapolis: University of Minnesota Press, 2016).

[5]Tsing, Anna, "Blasted Landscapes (and the Gentle Arts of Mushroom Picking)," in *The Multispecies Salon*, edited by Eben Kirksey (Durham: Duke University Press, 2020), 87-109.

[6]Yamada, Toshihiro, "Mushrooms: Radioactive Contamination of Widespread Mushrooms in Japan," *Agricultural Implications of the Fukushima*

Making clear that the abilities of fungi to remediate blasted landscapes in no way justifies human violence against the constituents of our shared planet, Tsing's hopefulness for a more collaborative, multispecies future is substantiated by Suzanne Simard's ecological research in the forests of nearby British Columbia.[7] Her findings explain how mycorrhizal fungal networks enhance the survivability of diverse forest participants by facilitating a multispecies communication and resource-sharing system. The moniker "wood-wide web" cutely describes how underground mycelia transfer messages, such as warnings, and resources, such as glucose, but the internet metaphor vastly oversimplifies the ecological responsibility that these mycelia have as they move biochemical signals and cellular fluids between trees and other plants.

However, as Merlin Sheldrake and many other ecologists have pointed out, the picture of Sherwood Forest with mycorrhiza as Robin Hood taking sugar from rich trees and giving it to poor ones is also overly simplistic.[8] Along with the capacity for learning, memory, and cognition that these

Nuclear Accident, edited by Tomoko M. Nakanishi and Keitaro Tanoi (Springer, 2013), 163-176.

[7]E.g., Simard, Suzanne W., "Mycorrhizal Networks Facilitate Tree Communication, Memory, Learning," *Memory and Learning in Plants*, edited by Frantisek Balusa, Monika Gagliano, and Guenther Witzany (Springer, 2018), 191-213.

[8]Sheldrake, *Entangled Life*, 160-162.

botanical and fungal organisms possess, they also have what we might call personalities. Some types of mycorrhizae are generous, nurturing, maybe even compassionate, and others are grouchy hoarders, greedy stockbrokers, or gluttons who build underground networks only to consume plant matter, not cooperate with it. None is a passive factotum doing trees' bidding, a socialist woodland referee, or an altruistic charity organization. Despite these more nuanced mycorrhizal Merry Men, it is undeniable that the biome of Sherwood Forest could not exist without its bustling, underground entanglements of fungi, each with its own agenda to push through the soil.

Ears to the Ground

Even while acknowledging their individual agency, mushrooms are increasingly harnessed by humans into a "heal the world" paradigm, hardly a fair partnership considering they aren't the ones responsible for the current extinction event. Mycologist Paul Stamets's book *Mycelium Running: How Mushrooms Can Help Save the World*, is one of the earlier cases in point.[9] There is a similar evangelical strain in Peter McCoy's *Radical Mycology*, where fungi are

---

[9]Stamets, Paul, *Mycelium Running: How Mushrooms Can Help Save the World* (Berkeley: Ten Speed Press, 2005).

purveyors of ancient wisdom, employed to teach us lessons about embodying "Nature's most refined principles" and "respecting and connecting with the natural world."[10] Following Stamets's push for "mycorestoration," the ability of fungi to revitalize the conditions for life is even exploited by NASA's myco-architecture project to help enable the colonization of Mars—the "planet B" just in case mushrooms can't save us on Earth after all.[11]

In Michael Marder's *Plant-Thinking*, his philosophy of vegetal life begins by decrying the human tendency to view plants solely in terms of what they can do for us. This utilitarian or instrumentalizing approach to encounters with the nonhuman is grounded in Hegelian philosophy: "The silent essence of self-less Nature in its fruits ... offers itself to life that has a self-like nature. In its usefulness as food and drink it reaches its highest perfection."[12] In this sense, as Marder notes, a forest is a passive entity awaiting its elevation to a purer state of usefulness to humankind. Trees ascend to a higher existence when they become pages

---

[10]McCoy, Peter, *Radical Mycology: A Treatise on Seeing and Working with Fungi* (Portland: Chthaeus Press, 2016), 1.

[11]Rothschild, Lynn, "Myco-Architecture off Planet: Growing Surface Structures at Destination," NASA, 30 March 2018; last accessed 20 August 2021 at https://www.nasa.gov/directorates/spacetech/niac/2018_Phase_I _Phase_II/Myco-architecture_off_planet/.

[12]Hegel, *Phenomenology of Spirit*, 436-437; quoted in Marder, *Plant-Thinking*, 26.

in a book, logs in a fireplace, or construction materials for a ship. Mushrooms find contact with spiritual reality by gracing our dinner plates, fighting our cancers, altering our consciousness, producing our penicillin, cleaning our polluted soil, rebuilding the biosphere we collapsed, teaching us lessons in eco-friendliness, and fabricating new homes for us elsewhere in the galaxy. One can easily see how this philosophy has failed us all.

On the other hand, Levi Bryant would suggest that the utilitarianism might go both ways.[13] From phenomenology of spirit to alien phenomenology, he explains how, from the perspective of Kentucky bluegrass, the plant has managed to seduce American lawn-owners into dispersing its seeds and increasing its kind all over the country, far beyond its endemic distribution. Likewise, if you were to ask cattle, they might think they're the more powerful agricultural player since the entire social ordering of American life, from food to fashion, revolves around them. They have seduced humans with their flesh to the point that they are granted predator-free, fenced-in fields with dedicated breeding grounds, or better yet, the less messy artificial insemination. The beef and dairy industries are dedicated entirely to ensuring the

---

[13]Bryant, Levi R, *Onto-Cartography: An Ontology of Machines and Media* (Edinburgh: Edinburgh University Press, 2014), 65-68. I made a similar argument about the *Cedrus* genus in Rich, Sara A., *Cedar Forests, Cedar Ships: Allure, Lore, and Metaphor in the Mediterranean Near East* (Oxford: Archaeopress, 2017).

healthy and frequent reproduction of cattle, which could be understood by them as an evolutionary boon.

Without suggesting that cattle are to blame for the environmental and public health crises that have resulted from our obsession with beef, Bryant's point is worth considering as we keep our ears to the ground, listening to the mushrooms. If we were to consider the various projects to which we subject fungi from their perspective, could a similar argument be made? Might fungi find such partnerships—which entail expanded spore and hyphae dispersal—a fair and just one after all?

Like an arranged marriage, bluegrass, cattle, and fungi might not have entered into partnerships with "man" willfully. But does consent matter outside our own genus? What about beyond our own kingdom? Canadian mycologist Harold Brodie thought so. His wonderful book, *Fungi: Delight of Curiosity*, was decades ahead of its time for insisting on the viewpoints of nonhuman others, in something similar to what Ian Bogost would later term alien phenomenology.

Brodie's book is laced with references to alchemist mycelia and the agency of raindrops, as he questions repeatedly why men tend to ignore nonhuman beings until they either intrude into what man perceives as his own realm, or they can be exploited for man's own benefit. He laments the anthropocentrism of the so-what question that scientists and humanists alike are often asked, claiming that when encountering fungal peculiarities, "little if any enlightenment is likely to come from a question involving the word 'meaning' (significance, purpose, use, or what you will)" because it depends on whom you ask: fungus, soil, plant, nematode, or man.[14] He concludes that "the good or use of any living thing does not depend solely upon whether or not it happens to fit into man's limited viewpoint." Things exist on their own terms, negotiated with others they encounter.

It seems at least possible that mycoremediation and mycofabrication are the latest efforts to trick other species into doing our bidding without heeding their terms and conditions. And, ethics aside for a moment, historically, such deception has backfired numerous times, as with the introduction of cane toads to eat sugarcane beetles or kudzu to slow soil erosion brought on by deforestation. We have repeatedly acted as the old lady in the nursery rhyme who swallowed the fly, and who then swallows a bird to catch the fly, and keeps swallowing larger and larger animals to catch the one she swallowed before ("perhaps she'll die!" ring true the lyrics). Even agriculture itself involved tricking boars, ibexes, and aurochs into providing us a constant food source, and that too has had immeasurable downstream consequences.

Beginning some ten thousand years ago, the domestication of livestock and poultry has wrought havoc to habitats on a global scale. Timothy Morton explains that the logic of agriculture, or agrilogistics, has guided all these ecological

---

[14]Brodie, Harold J., *Fungi: Delight of Curiosity* (Toronto: University of Toronto Press, 1978), 91. The quote from the following line is from p. 122.

missteps throughout the Holocene.[15] The prevailing idea that when it comes to existence, quantity is better than quality, has undoubtedly led to our current ecocidal regime. And fungiculture, as a function of agriculture, is part of this inheritance: for example, the cultivation and administration of *Penicillium* sp. fungus-derived antibiotics resulted in an unprecedented global human population explosion, which is now prompting colonization beyond our home planet.

That said, other animals practice fungiculture too. Some ants, termites, beetles, and even periwinkles cultivate fungi in mutualistic farming partnerships. Having been raised on a small farm, the idea of mutualistic farming is particularly appealing to me. More importantly, it may offer a departure from Morton's agrilogistics and Tsing's plantation science, both of which identify modern human interactions with land, water, and their occupants as domineering if not parasitic.[16] Surely we can use our big brains and capacity for altruism to approach potential partnerships with nonhuman others by seeing things from their viewpoint, negotiating without deception, even treating them like kin. Surely, with ears kept to the ground, we can keep mutualism in mind.

* * *

---

[15]Morton, Timothy, *Dark Ecology* (New York: Columbia University Press, 2016); *Humankind* (London: Verso, 2017).
[16]Morton, *Dark Ecology* and *Humankind*; Tsing, "Blasted Landscapes," 201.

The other day, I spotted a fox squirrel among a remnant patch of longleaf pines. Longleaf pine forests once covered much of the American Southeast, but European settlers, timber barons, and plantation owners cleared those forests, and with their demise went entire ecosystems. With their preferred habitat continuing to decline, so do the numbers of lovely fox squirrels. Come to find out, fox squirrels eat hypogeous fungi, or underground mushrooms, that form the mycorrhizal network for longleaf pines. As they gallivant through the forest defecating fungal spores, fox squirrels spread mycelia, which in turn help facilitate the growth and sustain the health of the pines. In return, pines offer tree cavities in which the squirrels might safely rear their young. There is a three-way mutualism between plant, fungus, and animal. Without one, the other two suffer.

Writing after the Second World War, English botanist M. C. Rayner was among the first to determine the extent of mycorrhizal mutualisms. She, however, generously shares this credit with 19th-century German botanist A. B. Frank, whom she quotes as having described fungal mycelia as "the foster-mothers of the trees."[17] Falling headlong into the woven snare of anthropomorphism, this metaphor has the advantage of suggesting the kind of care that extends to entities outside one's immediate family. I've recently become

---

[17]Rayner, M. C., *Trees and Toadstools* (Emmaus, Pennsylvania: Rodale Press, 1947), 52.

step-mother to two young girls, and this kind of intra-family care comes with all manners of challenges and joys, impossible to anticipate. It's hard to help raise someone else's children, and foster- and step-mothers are probably universally undervalued for their social contributions. So too are the foster-mothers of the trees, who balance—sometimes imperfectly—their own ambitions and desires with the task of facilitating the growth and sustaining the health of the woodland family.

SPRING

Morel
Dutch: *morielje*
French: *morille*
Latin: *Morchella* sp.

Stemming from proto-Germanic sources meaning "edible root," this mushroom's most commonplace common name fails to betray its outstanding flavor. This is the mushroom most frequently sought by foragers in the Northern Hemisphere. Its appearance is distinctive, with a cap defined by the folds, ruffles, and pleats of a Flamenco dancer's dress rather than the smooth skin or papery lamella of other toadstools. But instead of satiny reds, this Flamenco dancer wears the earthy browns and greys of someone in hiding or otherwise expressing modesty or anonymity.

Morels are one of the few edibles to fruit in spring, sometimes even before winter's end. Generally, they can be found growing on the ground, from smooth upright stalks, beneath hardwood trees, although some species prefer conifers or mixed stands. There is some evidence that morels, or at least certain species, prefer soils in woodlands whose underbrush has recently been cleared by fire. White morels notoriously grow near dead or dying elm trees, which can provide a site to return to season after season. Morels range in height from an inch to over a foot tall, and they grow in singles or in groups. The guidebooks sometimes use the word "gregarious" to describe them, which I believe after my own step-mother collected an unusually large congregation of 53 near the creek, beneath a giant fallen elm, on my family land in Kansas early last year.

Dangerous lookalikes are also plentiful, but watchful scrutiny can root out the edibles. True morels have hollow caps and stipes, unlike their imposters. Those hollow caps and stipes are both edible, so use a sharp knife to cut at the base, above the soil line, and harvest the entire mushroom without overly damaging the mycelium to which the stipe is attached in the soil.

There are numerous ways to prepare and preserve the harvest. They can be sautéed, added to soups and casseroles, or battered and fried. Leftovers can be preserved by cooking and then freezing, or by drying and then reconstituting with water when the need arises. Preserving will not compromise flavor, rather to the contrary. If the temperature and humidity are controlled, you can even run a thread through the stalks and hang them upside down as you would line-drying a load of laundry. The soft folds and pleats will eventually dry and harden, at which point you can remove them from their garland and place them in an airtight container for later enjoyment.

PART IV

MEDICINE

Correspondence

If one looks closely, there are sharp, rebellious, points of contrast to the prevailing 19th-century European conception of lifeforms neatly stacked on a staircase headed up to God in heaven. In his 1857 poem "Correspondances," Charles Baudelaire describes an earthy mysticism that pervades all things equally, and of which humans are only a small, unwitting, part.

La Nature est un temple où de vivants piliers
Laissent parfois sortir de confuses paroles;
L'homme y passe à travers des forêts de symbols
Qui l'observent avec des regards familiers.

Comme de longs échos qui de loin se confondent
Dans une ténébreuse et profonde unité,
Vaste comme la nuit et comme la clarté,
Les parfums, les couleurs et les sons se répondent.

Il est des parfums frais comme des chairs d'enfants,
Doux comme les hautbois, verts comme les prairies,
—Et d'autres, corrompus, riches et triomphants,

Ayant l'expansion des choses infinies,
Comme l'ambre, le musc, le benjoin et l'encens,
Qui chantent les transports de l'esprit et des sens.

Nature is a temple where living columns
Sometimes whisper strange words;
Man passes through forests of symbols
Who observe him with a familiar gaze.

As merging echoes from beyond
Through a tenebrous and deep unity,
Vast as the night and the epiphany of day
The aromas, the colors, the sounds, they correspond.

It is the fresh smell of a baby's skin,
Sweet like a woodwind, green as the prairies,
And others, corrupt, rich and victorious,

With the expansion of infinite things,
Like amber, musk, resin, and incense,
Who sing away the spirit and the senses.

Baudelaire's animated world is infused with the resinous smell of opium drifting through talking trees and all-seeing vines, some affable and others greedy or vain. This eerie forest of *choses infinies* is replete with things who don't just bustle, but watch, know, and sense, and those senses and spirits mingle and merge with each other in a ceaseless dance of leading and following, taking and giving.

With this mystical high in mind, here is another piece of advice from my dad: only use drugs that grow from the ground. A child of the 60s, he would know. Of course, one could argue that hard drugs like heroin and cocaine also grow from the ground, but I knew what he meant. Stick to the ones that still resemble their original form, like marijuana and mushrooms. In college at the University of Kansas, where I was studying fine art, I stuck to his advice, mostly. Once I was tripping on mushrooms while walking with my canine companion, Sophia, and we came across a dead opossum. Guts spilled like strewn glitter, lips spread in a perpetual smile—it was the saddest, most beautiful thing I'd ever seen. That roadkill marsupial was a breakthrough for me, and I still rarely produce visual art that doesn't involve faunal remains of some kind.

Another time, Rani and Lara (my college roommates) and I were feeling the effects of metabolized psilocybin, so we took a cartoon-version of Sophia—who was privy to 14 years of my youthful indiscretions—to a park with a wading pool. I climbed the fence and drifted through the pool, entirely clothed. The tepid, chlorinated water on my skin was glorious—I can still almost feel it now, nearly twenty years later, gliding through and gilded by molten electrum. And then came the police. I scaled the fence, but my skirt caught on the chain-link and ripped on the way down. The officer was so embarrassed that he just told us to go home, and we did, laughing the whole way in an animated alt-world.

Although popularly called "magic mushrooms," the hallucinogenic properties of psilocybin are now widely recognized for their therapeutic potentials. Shrooms stimulate raucous laughter, open new ways of seeing, reroute old patterns of thinking, and by encouraging a sense of connectedness, they reframe one's sense of place in a vast and unknowable universe. From psychedelic to psychiatric drug, psilocybin is successfully treating war veterans with PTSD and sufferers of severe depression. Recalling the metaphorical potentials for mushrooming, the serotonin-like substance stimulates nerve cell regrowth in the parts of the brain associated with memory and emotion.

Members of the globally distributed genus *Psilocybe* have been used for hundreds if not thousands of years to resolve all manners of health concerns. But between the colonial fear surrounding Indigenous ceremonial applications and the spread of recreational drug use among anti-war beatniks and hippies, the Nixon administration banned psilocybin and psilocin as dangerous substances. Following the 1970 Controlled Substances Act, the US Food and Drug Administration (FDA) shut down scientific inquiry into the medical potentials of magic mushrooms and their ilk, and several other countries followed suit. Although bound to be highly regulated, there is now some promise for hallucinogens to resume a little of their precolonial status as healers of mind and soul.

Although a differentiation between mind, soul, and body is dubious, neither is the body beyond the healing powers of fungi. Reishi, shiitake, and maitake mushrooms have all been popularized recently as panaceas for fatigue, immunodeficiency, and even obesity and cancer. Based on testing with mice, maitake (also known as hen-of-the-woods), Brazilian almond mushrooms, and lion's mane have displayed antimicrobial and anti-inflammatory properties that may assist in the treatment of COVID-19 patients.

As numerous publications in the *International Journal on Medicinal Mushrooms* and elsewhere can attest, these and other medicinal mushrooms have longstanding pharmaceutical traditions among non-Western and pre-Modern medical practitioners, so these tentative clinical confirmations are of no great surprise to many. Ötzi the Iceman carried the inedible birch polypore—along with some tinder fungus and stone and bone tools—in a sheepskin sack on his belt, most likely for its antimicrobial, antiparasitic, anti-inflammatory, and analgesic properties when used as a tincture or infusion. The underneath side of the mushroom can also be used as a bandage to halt bleeding and prevent infection. Five thousand years later, and the Copper Age first-aid kit is still used in parts of Eastern Europe. Now that the efficacy of this ancient and folk remedy has been verified by laboratory science, birch polypore is cultivated and numerous supplement companies are producing extracts for sale on the internet.

The commodification of medicinals has at least one dark side. The mushroom *Cordyceps sinensis* is endemic to the Himalayan plateaus of India, Tibet, Nepal, Bhutan, and China. The fungus is a flagship species that indicates the health of the alpine meadows, and its presence has been tied to dozens of plant and animal species that compose this delicate ecosystem. Known as the caterpillar fungus, it is parasitic like its close relative, the zombie ant fungus described earlier. This fungus infects ghost moth larvae growing in the soil overwinter, uses their bodies as hosts before killing and mummifying them, and then in spring, it sends up through the head of the dead larva a spore-bearing stalk, which is visible to foragers aboveground as the head of a narrow if rather erect 5 to 6-inch phallus. The mushroom, and the caterpillar through which it grows, has been used in Chinese and Vedic medicine for centuries to cure what ails— and for many, what ails is the libido. However, increased global awareness of this ancient aphrodisiac has led to over-exploitation, endangering the fungus population and the alpine ecosystem of which it is an integral part.

Like the European aphrodisiac *Phallus impudicus*, it was initially due to the visual similarities between respective reproductive organs of fungus and human male that *C. sinensis* has long been the preferred treatment for low sex drives and erectile dysfunction in South and East Asia. But unlike *P. impudicus*, recent clinical trials have lent considerable scientific credence to the medical traditions involving the caterpillar fungus, which began as a category of sympathetic magic known as "correspondence."

In his multi-volume tome *The Golden Bough*, first published in 1889, Sir James George Frazier articulated the concept of "sympathetic magic" as a kind of magical thinking with two subcategories: correspondence and contagion.[1] While contagion pertains to objects that have made physical contact with the recipient of the magic, correspondence involves imitation, or the principle of "like begets like"; for example, a painting of a deceased loved one that transmits messages from beyond the grave, a performance that enacts a desired effect in reality, or the consumption of phallic-shaped mushrooms to enhance sexual activity.

Correspondence has endured in folk medicine, as seen with the wisdom that kidney beans are good for your kidneys because they are shaped like their eponymous organ, or walnuts look like a brain, so you should eat walnuts to enhance your thinking. As it turns out, occasionally the old wives knew what they were talking about without the aid of a microscope or lab mice. Regular walnut consumption does enhance cognitive function, and kidney beans do support kidney health and prevent kidney stones.

---

[1]Frazier, James George. *The Golden Bough: A Study in Magic and Religion* (New York: MacMillan Company, 1925), 11.

Of course, all these medicinal foods that resemble their intended organ—brain, kidney, or phallus—do far more than merely seek out and bolster their corporeal counterpart. The chemical compounds aiding those specific organs also help maintain the health of other bodily mechanisms, like the heart, liver, skin, and blood. Yet, despite some spurious base assumptions, there is a logic to sympathetic magic. As anthropologist Michael Taussig explains, correspondence works by way of complex and often sophisticated analogies between comparable entities, so that the means and ends are not dissimilar to applied science.[2] Natural laws would appear to govern sequences of events so that they become explicable, replicable, and predictable. And because of some 5,000 years of explication, replicability, and predictability, the bioactive compounds of the phallus-shaped aphrodisiac *C. sinensis* are now produced in laboratories, supplying global demand while sparing some of the alpine populations and their ecological partners.

One the one hand, it may seem as though medical science is simply trying to catch up to traditional medicine. But besides mimicking polymers through artificial replication, and thus leaving more fungal habitats in place, science also has the advantage of being able to better explain why certain mushrooms remediate certain ailments. Yet, as we

---

[2]Taussig, Michael. *Mimesis and Alterity: A Particular History of the Senses* (New York and London: Routledge, 1993), 43.

consider all the potentials for beneficial polysaccharides found in medicinal mushrooms, we are again faced with the problem of *telos*, the function or usefulness of a thing. Cultivated in test tubes, compounds isolated, juices extracted and concentrated—to a Hegelian, it might seem that this fungus has been elevated to a higher purpose than merely parasitizing moth larvae in some Tibetan meadow. But all that has been elevated is the artificial preeminence of human health above all else.

The idea that all the stuff out there in the world is passively waiting for us to first, discover it, and second, figure out how to use that discovery to make our lives a little easier, is deeply and ethically flawed. Unfortunately, this idea has also been a core feature of scientific endeavors for hundreds of years. We might do well to note that the word "data" is derived from the Latin *dare*, to give. Data are gifts, not discoveries. And like my grandma used to say, you shouldn't look a gift horse in the mouth. Following this sage wisdom, we might accept, with good grace, what the world offers, "rather than attempting to extract—whether by force or subterfuge—what it does not."[3]

In the introduction to *Correspondences*, anthropologist Tim Ingold reminds us that when we observe a thing—the first step in all scientific inquiry—what we see is "the stone in its stoning, the tree in its arborescence, the mountain in its rising and falling," and of course the mushroom

---

[3]Ingold, Tim, *Correspondences* (Cambridge: Polity, 2021), 10.

in its mushrooming. Like Robin Wall Kimmerer, he too recommends that we replace all our nouns for naming things with verbs: to stone, to tree, to mountain, to mushroom. With verbs, we see things in action, resisting clear-cut classification, reverberating with each other while differentiating from each other. Things are their stories of reverberation and differentiation, and within each story, there is also the story of those differentiated from it: moss, bird, mountaineer, forager. The constituents of lichen who recognize difference before compatibility would seem to be a case in point.

For Ingold, correspondence is a process of carefully attending to fellow earthlings, contemplating passing observations and fleeting encounters. As in writing letters to an old friend or someone you've never even met, correspondence requires care, time, patience, and anticipation. Correspondence is an unfolding dialogue crafted with another, foreign or familiar. In this way, the great chain of being snaps and becomes a great chain letter of becoming, which goes on-and-on, back-and-forth, open-endedly. Maybe you get something back, maybe you don't.

Besides exchanging verbs for nouns, there is another way that Ingold's correspondence resonates with Kimmerer's writing. She muses on the Onondaga Thanksgiving Address, or The Words That Come Before All Else, as it is given before school starts each day in Onondaga Nation in upstate New York. Unlike the obligatory Pledge of Allegiance recited in public schools across America, the Thanksgiving Address is not a pledge, prayer, or poem as much as it is an invocation of gratitude to Earth and all her constituents: waters, winds, fish, plants, berries, herbs, trees, animals, sun, stars, teachers, creator. Each receives thanks for the gifts bestowed upon the people, and with the conclusion of each address comes the words "now our minds are one."[4]

Kimmerer goes on to reason that duties and gifts are one and the same. We might say, then, that duties and data are one and the same. Our gift is our responsibility, and certainly intelligence is one of those gifts. But since humans are also notably gifted with the capacity for gratitude, showing it is also both gift and responsibility. So let us pledge reciprocity with the living world, Kimmerer says. Let our allegiance be to the democracy of the species, to the land herself, and if justice is to prevail, let it be justice truly for all.

Let the gift of our data give back.

Saint Children

As I write this section on medicinal mushrooms, my eyes keep straying over to the small buckskin pouch hanging above my desk. Inside this pouch, there are representatives of the plant, animal, mineral, extraterrestrial, and cultural realms, in accordance with Waccamaw tradition. While the

---

[4]Kimmerer, *Braiding Sweetgrass*, 105-117.

specifics of its contents are private, I have added a fungal component too.

The medicine bag was a gift from Chief Hatcher, and one that I cherish. As I child, I had another leather pouch, that one beaded and fringed, with various contents as sacred to a ten-year-old as they could be. The animal component was given to me by a member of the Kansas Munsee, but I'm not sure where the bag itself came from. At any rate, I regarded that little pouch with odds and ends as my medicine bag and took it with me on all my horse rides (first with Judy, then Amigo) around the countryside. Its whereabouts now are unknown, perhaps discarded in the aftermath of religious conversion and the purging of all things pagan. No wonder I hold Chief's gift so dear.

But I do wonder about the Indigenous American concept of medicine, and how it might play out in a place that has so much healing to do. Medicine—akin to luck, karma, or mana—is a kind of cosmic power that issues from certain objects and actions. Medicine is a neutral permeating force that can be cultivated or charged into a positive or negative, depending on the effect or the intent. A gift given out of love is good medicine, whereas that same gift given begrudgingly might be bad medicine. Given the nature of data, the implications are as clear for science as for spirituality.

The medicine wheel, or sacred circle, identifies the distribution of this fundamental force. But it is more than a diagram or map; it is a microcosm of the physical and spiritual universes and the individual's role in them, which communicates how these realms of self and more-than-self correspond. The circle, itself representative of the boundary between earth and sun, is divided into quadrants, each corresponding to a color (red, yellow, black, white), a cardinal direction, a season, a type of being (plant, animal, human, mineral), a time of day (dawn, noon, dusk, midnight), a branch of healing (mental, physical, emotional, spiritual). These categories and their locations on the circle differ between cultures, but each variation is meant to act as a guide for how distinct elements in the world relate to each other, and how we relate to them to ensure the continued circulation of good medicine between all cosmic constituents.

At the Waccamaw Fire Ceremony, the fire is in the center of a large circle demarcated with a wooden fence, painted in four colors for the four cardinal directions. The circle itself is located near the center of tribal grounds. To welcome this most recent autumn equinox, there were only a few of us there for the sunrise ceremony. We each took a handful of sage and tobacco, entered the circle, and offered a pinch of the tobacco and sage to each of the cardinal directions, starting with the east, in the direction of the rising sun, and moving clockwise around the circle. Each quadrant of the sacred circle received its acknowledgement, and each movement was meditative, meaningful, medicinal. This process was repeated at noon, when more were in attendance, with the addition of a spoken component on the significance of the fire at the circle's center, and what it meant to each of us. Chief spoke of the fire as a continuation of his people's traditions that, despite genocide, erasure, and assimilation, can never fully be extinguished.

Indigenous Mesoamerican traditions have likewise struggled to keep burning in the aftermath of 500 years of Spanish colonization. Nestled in the Oaxacan Mountains, somewhere between the Mazatec and Christian worldviews, traditional healer María Sabina lamented the arrival of foreigners, "young people, blond and dark-skinned," to her doorstep.[5] She was not speaking of colonizers in the traditional sense, but tourists from the United States and Europe who had come for her medicine. They asked to be cured, to be shown God. She brought them into her vigils, orderly and in keeping with Mazatec tradition, which crucially involved the ingestion of "saint children," or hallucinogenic psilocybin mushrooms. All participants in the vigil consumed the mushrooms to access the spirit realm and its wisdom. But the foreigners abused the custom. They took the mushrooms at her vigils under false pretenses, disrespected the taboos of gathering and eating them, and henceforth, the saint children began to lose their power. Toward the end of her life in 1985, she remarked that for the spoiling of the saint children, there was no remedy.

The same drive among the foreigners to exploit the children and the healer has resulted in an entirely predictable

---

[5] María Sabina, *Selections*, edited by Jerome Rothenberg (Berkeley: University of California Press, 2003).

outcome, one which María Sabina likely foresaw decades ago; indeed, this outcome in its incipience may even have been what sent some foreigners running desperately into her candlelit vigils, seeking psychedelic relief. Writing some 10 years after the healer's death, Rodney Harrison coined the term "species loneliness" to describe the condition in which we moderns and postmoderns have flung ourselves: "Precisely at the moment when we have overcome the earth and become unearthly in our modes of dwelling, precisely when we are on the verge of becoming cyborgs, we insist on our kinship with the animate world."[6] Will the animate world accept us back, prodigal and revenant? I'm not sure I would if I were her. But then again, I am something of a shameless misanthrope, a self-loathing human in the new geological era of our own making, the Misanthropocene. My pessimism needs a cure.

Luckily, she is far more generous and gracious than I. When I spoke at the Fire Ceremony, I said something about the balancing of logs to build a fire, the equinox being a moment of balance between day and night, and the need to restore ecological balance by looking to Indigenous models of stewardship. My eyes grew hot and my voice broke. Smoke circled skyward, as heat from the burning logs spread through the soil, radiant in all directions.

---

[6]Rodney Harrison. "Toward a Philosophy of Nature." In *Uncommon Ground: Rethinking the Human Place in Nature*, edited by W. Cronon, 426-437 (New York: W.W. Norton, 1996), 428.

Medicine circulates: I am reminded this autumn with every circle of a mushroom cap, a round bundle of ringless honeys, or a fairy ring of blewits or even vomiters. Circles within circles, sacred perhaps, corresponding with secret negotiations between beings unseen.

Like most if not all postcolonial tribal communities, religious beliefs among the Waccamaw are incredibly diverse. And so I have a non-confession: I am not a traditionalist. I don't believe in the Grandfather, the Creator, the Great Spirit. I see smoke drifting upward, where others might see it being welcomed by a superior being. But my attention returns to the ground. I see that fire ring spreading down into the earth, heating the soil and all those who live in it. To me, that is more significant. That wet, dark circle, hot and pulsing with life, is what feeds all things.

Step into that sacred circle, that *hexenkring*, that *rond des sorcières*. That circle is fertile, and not just in the fetal way. Following Mary Daly directly into its center, she implores all women to re-become witches. We have a legacy of healing, midwifery, and wisdom that patriarchal forces (churches, states, universities, families) have tried in vain to eradicate. We, the Hags, might tap into this legacy and witness Earth remedying herself, while we look for ways to help her as much as we can. There's so much healing to do, so much bringing-into-the-world to be done, so much wisdom needed.

While Daly calls on her fellow females to take the torch and light the gallows ablaze, Kimmerer wonders if a settler colony, full of immigrants, could ever share the sense of rootedness to the land and water that Indigenous peoples have as a birthright.[7] Can immigrants indigenize? She concludes that by "honoring the knowledge in the land, and caring for its keepers, we start to become Indigenous to place." Reasoning by analogy, there are invasive species that consume everything in their path—garlic mustard, kudzu, mimosa—but there are also alien species who become naturalized—dandelions, plantain—who live in reciprocity with their fellows and the land, offering medicinal value along the way. Naturalization is not just a legal process or citizenship status but a process that is at once ecological, ethical, spiritual, and medicinal, maybe. Kimmerer explains:

> Being naturalized to place means to live as if this is the land that feeds you, as if these are the streams from which you drink, that build your body and fill your spirit. To become naturalized is to know that your ancestors lie in this ground. Here you will give your gifts and meet your responsibilities. To become naturalized is to live as if your children's future matters, to take care of the land as if our lives and the lives of all our relatives depend on it. Because they do.[8]

With these dual calls to action—Hags to witch and settlers to naturalize—a crooked path into the sacred circle of mushroom metaphysics is opened. Will you follow it?

---

[7] Kimmerer, *Braiding Sweetgrass*, 210.
[8] Kimmerer, *Braiding Sweetgrass*, 215.

SUMMER

Puffball
Dutch: *bovist*; *stuifzwam*
French: *vesse-de-loup*; *tête de mort*
Latin: *Calvatia gigantia* and *Lycoperdon perlatum*

This fascinating group of mushrooms looks exactly like what their various names would suggest. Although diverse in appearance, what they share in common is their incubation of spores inside their flesh, and at their coming-of-age moment, the flesh at the top of the cap bursts open and dusty spores erupt into the air, slowly drifting down to the earth to await their own coming-of-age.

The giant puffball (*C. gigantia*) is a white, spherical mushroom with no stalk to speak of; rather, it attaches to the ground by way of something resembling a tiny golf tee with roots. The puffball itself can be the size of a golf ball or a volleyball with the makings for many meals. The young ones are white inside and out, and those are the only ones that should be harvested. Use a knife to cut a small sample of the flesh and make sure it is white all the way through. If so, use the knife again and cut the puffball at its base horizontally an inch or so above the ground to avoid damage to the mycelium.

Another variety of puffball, sometimes known as the devil's snuff-box (*L. perlatum*), is also a common edible. It has a thick stalk from which the cap never separates, giving it a club-like profile. It has a spiky-looking but soft-feeling texture at the top of the cap. These puffballs should be checked and harvested the same way as the related giants, and others of their kind.

I have foraged both these mushrooms and their close relatives from my back yard and in front of tree lines. They prefer open, sunny spots like meadows and lawns. To prepare them, it is recommended to remove the tough outer layer of skin before cooking or preserving. The flesh has a soft texture, like nougat or tofu, and is excellent in pasta dishes. To toughen the texture, pan-fry before adding to the dish. Leftovers can be preserved by simply dicing into cubes and freezing.

PART V

MAGIC

Sacrificial Victims

Painted by Matthias Grünewald in 1516, the Isenheim altarpiece is a wondrous work of magic whose doors open and close to reveal the ultimate story of sacrifice: this is the Christ invoked by María Sabina's chants during her candlelit healing missions in Oaxaca. This is Christ nearly dead, the Christ who knows what it means to suffer. The Christ who is dead, stretched in rigor mortis and bespeckled with seeping, gangrenous wounds. But also, the Christ who is vaulted into a technicolor sky, triumphant in hallucinated heavens. María knew this Christ well.

The thaumaturgical altarpiece was commissioned by the Isenheim hospital, run by the Brothers of St. Anthony. The monks specialized in treating St. Anthony's fire, a disease caused by the fungus ergot (*Claviceps purpurea*), which hides out in grains like rye and gets ground up into flour and baked into bread then eaten unwittingly. St. Anthony's curative powers rendered him the patron saint of ergotism, as he worked his miracles to alleviate symptoms of gangrenous sores, powerful hallucinations, gastrointestinal bloating, and convulsions. Some speculate that Grünewald himself had once suffered and recovered from ergotism; how else could he have known to paint those hallucinations so faithfully?

The altarpiece displays St. Anthony tempted by a monstrous personification of the disease, but it is Christ who suffers and dies from it. When the doors with the crucified, fungus-stricken god were opened, a fellow ergot-poisoned sufferer would witness the stone lid of His sarcophagus tossed aside as the holy corpse is reborn, airborne, stigmata held skyward and levitating toward the great golden fireball that will whisk Him back to heaven. The fellow sufferer might rest assured, knowing that pain and death are temporary, and when his body can no longer take the poison, he will join Christ on that fireball and rocket from his crypt into the sky. What solace there is in sacrifice!

From ergotamine, an alkaloid contained in ergot, lysergic acid is derived, which in turn is used to synthesize lysergic acid diethylamide, otherwise known as LSD (or acid). When the doors of perception are flung far open, as with those of the Isenheim altarpiece and the Nazarene's coffin, technicolor dreams threaten to come true. Cosmic secrets reveal themselves. Mysterious things start to make sense. Magic happens.

More than sleight of hand or smoke and mirrors, fungal magic does not just deal in perception and its limits. There is a physicality, not just a physiology, to fungal arts. Perhaps the best example of baffling escape artistry that is no mere illusion is found in bird's nest fungi (*Nidularia* and related genera).[1] Resembling tiny nests, these mushrooms grow on rotting wood and dung. Each fragile fungal nest harbors dozens of eggs, called peridioles, which are filled not with yolk but spores. The expectant nest waits patiently. These eggs will not hatch without help. Clouds form and gather. Rain falls. A single raindrop hits the perfect spot inside the nest to form a spectacular if minuscule waterspout. The peridioles are vaulted out of the nest like Jesus from his crypt, flying through the air not in ascension to heaven but descension earthward. The sticky peridiole attaches to a leaf or blade of grass, and the soft shell opens. Spores escape to the earth, or in some cases, the foliage to which the peridiole was stuck is eaten, and spores pass through the herbivore's digestive system, landing far away from their nest in a pile of soft, warm dung. And the cycle repeats, as the circle of birds' nests patiently, steadily grows its circumference, one raindrop, one spore, one hypha, one bowel movement at a time.

---

[1] Brodie, *Fungi*, 51-58.

None of this is magic, you may argue. The Isenheim altarpiece with its psychedelic acid Jesus is religion, and bird's nest fungi with their water-gun-flung spores is science. Move along, no magic to be found here.

But it is there, hidden, slyly averting discovery. This is the thing for which we forage.

All three practices or crafts—magic, religion, science—are rooted in our incapacity for complete comprehension of the world and how we exist as a part of it. As feminist theologian Mary Daly points out, "craft" and "crave" share etymologies, so that behind every craft, there is a craving—a foraging, perhaps.[2] Science uses knowns to explain unknowns, as data come out from hiding, exposing themselves as givens, revealing their long-kept phenomenal secrets. Rather than following in Galen's path of interrogation by means of torture, science at its best hears secrets told willingly. And yet, the more we learn through science, the more we are like Socrates, increasingly aware of how little we really know. Every research question answered raises a thousand more. The gaping wound of wonder is opened, a stigma into which doubting Thomas might stick a finger.

Where science opens inquiry, religion has a reputation for shutting it down. Aphorisms abound: The Lord works in mysterious ways. Trust in the Lord and lean not on your own understanding. Do not partake of fruit from the Tree of

---

[2] Daly, *Gyn/Ecology*, xxvi.

Knowledge. Kill them all and let the knowing God sort them out (*Caedite eos. Novit enim Dominus qui sunt eius.*). The pious are left closing off wonder so as not to overstep their mortal bounds. Fear and wonder should be directed solely toward that inscrutable God, who keeps knowledge under lock and key, sin and serpent.

In their own way, both religion and science affirm the limits of human knowledge. Some things are simply beyond our knowing, cast into that beyond by either dogma or biology. The difference lies in how they each regard the unknown or the unknowable: for science, it is an invitation; for religion, a taboo. And so in this way, science might have more in common with magic, as they both truly crave Mystery's exposure rather than shying from it. Science and magic fling open the doors of perception with heathenish abandon.

At the same time, magic and religion are notoriously difficult to disentangle. Anthropologists and theologians have been trying for decades, but there are always exceptions that make bifurcated categorization seemingly impossible. For a long time, any monotheistic spiritual practice was considered a religion, while polytheistic or animistic practices were relegated to the category of myth and magic. Magic was conceived as some kind of rudimentary form of religion, and with enough time or assimilation, heathenry would grow more complex and organized until it would eventually be promoted to the status of full-fledged religion—all the better if it resembled the one endorsed by the dominant people group. In postcolonial times, we have supposedly learned the error of this thinking. After all, when the tables are turned, it is clear that magic and magical thinking underscore much religious thought, regardless of how organized and powerful the religion in question. What is the difference between a prayer and an invocation? A miracle and a spell successfully cast? A priest and a shaman? The difference is that religion is what *we* practice; magic is what *they* practice.

But maybe there are other differences yet. Many religions, organized and powerful or marginalized and diffuse, require blood sacrifice. María Sabina split the breast of a chick before each vigil with the saint children. Aztec sacrificial offerings ranged from butterflies to jaguars and humans, who may have been pumped full of shrooms (called *teonanacatl*, meaning "divine mushroom" or "dangerous mushroom" in Nahuatl) before having their hearts cut out with an obsidian knife. Dogs were sacrificed in China, Siberia, Greece, and Hungary. Abraham/Ibrahim was willing to cut the throat of his son Isaac/Ismael at God's request, and during Eid al-Adha, millions of Muslims every year sacrifice an animal to commemorate the patriarch's obedience. Christ sacrificed his own life to reverse the Edenic curse.

In each case, the sacrifice was made to ingratiate a jealous god; in the case of Christianity, the angered god and the sacrificial victim were one and the same. Despite variations on this theme evident from the Neolithic to the present day, sacrifices apparently indicate a widespread idea that blood is the life force that satiates the Divine, which it returns by granting new life or other favors. And this is where magic and religion may separate: while religion is devoted to at least one higher power, magic is not, necessarily. Magical practices fundamentally acknowledge a mysterious permutation of at least one invisible force throughout all beings without necessarily being theistic. The invisible force or forces are powerful without necessarily reigning supreme, which is why the magical practitioner can often exhibit a certain amount of control over said forces through semiotic reasoning, coercing, or bartering with them. Fundamentally, magic, like science, is atheistic, independent of a supreme being or ultimate creator. And so in that respect, maybe the old colonizers were right, and magic is the mere rudiment of religion. Because all magic really needs is consciousness—no blood, no martyrs, no lords.

An overemphasis on bloodshed as sacrifice can only be the product of a longstanding ontological hierarchy that places animal life on a level above other kinds. The plant crops sacrificed by Cain were inadequate to the Lord. What would have happened had Cain sacrificed bloodless but beautiful gemstones? Or the sweetest waters of a faraway spring? Or a basket of choice edible mushrooms? God's scorn would still have sent him into a jealous rage, ironically resembling evermore He in whose image he was made. When Cain spilled Abel's blood, he seemed to be asking, "Is that good enough for you now?"

The god of capital, too, has been thanklessly receiving blood sacrifices for hundreds of years, and like all jealous gods, he keeps demanding more and more. But what will happen when "cheap nature" runs out, and the sacrifices of those residing in woodlands and waterways, coops and corrals, come at too high a cost to keep slaking the throat of this bloodthirsty god?[3] When such sacrifice is finally acknowledged for the waste that it is, toxified wastelands and wastewaters might recede, unveiling a powerful Earth who flourishes of her own accord. The mushrooms will preside as they always do in the aftermath of ecocide.

After fifty years of mycological and botanical research, Elias Fries wrote "in the evening of his life" that "the fungi have always above all been near to my heart. . . . So then I recommend the study of them to botanists living in the country as a lasting source of pleasure and of admiration for the wisdom which governs all nature."[4] This sentiment, penned by a kindly old scientist in 1857 (the same year Baudelaire wrote "Correspondances"), reflects the Enlightenment era scientific enterprise to know the Creator by studying the Creation. But what if our pleasure and admiration were directed not toward an omnipotent omniscience but toward the individual objects that elicit these feelings of joy and wonder—the true "delights of curiosity"?[5] In other words, what if there is no ultimate wisdom, and no supreme ruler?

---

[3]On cheap nature, see Moore, Jason W., *Capitalism in the Web of Life: Ecology and the Accumulation of Capital* (London and New York: Verso, 2015).
[4]Fries, *Autobiography*, 148.
[5]This is in reference to the subtitle of Brodie's book *Fungi: Delight of Curiosity*.

By subtle contrast to religion's need for a god to receive adoration and sacrifice, all magic needs is consciousness, and that we have in abundance. Akin to medicine, mana, luck, and karma, the ancient Greek concept of τύχη refers to an extrahuman force embedded in things, and actions that can work for or against human desires. It is not necessarily wise, and it is rarely just. It haphazardly brings fortune and misfortune, alters one's lot in life for better or worse, and takes chances with chaos and order. Like mycelial agents in a crowded wood, it is the negotiation that happens between all things, all the time. Humans, who are just hedging their bets, are but one thing among many, and in this whimsical court, our appeals are rarely heard because it is fungi who form the firmament here.

And they know it. While knowledge is not the same as the wisdom to which Fries refers, fungi know their powers despite the absence of a brain, just like they sense without eyes, nose, ears, tongue, or skin. They sense, and they respond. If agency is a marker of consciousness, we are forced to admit that not only are fungi conscious, but so too are plants, slime molds, bacteria, and viruses, who communicate sensations, decisions, and strategies, and who can solve problems altruistically.[6] It might even be concluded that they maintain

---

[6] See arguments in Bayne, Tim, 2013, "Agency as a Marker of Consciousness," eds. Andy Clark, Julian Kiverstein and Tillman Vierkant, *Decomposing the Will* (New York: Oxford University Press), 160-180.

a level of dignity, in that they form their own laws to govern their actions. This would mean, according to Immanuel Kant's *Groundwork for the Metaphysics of Morals*, that these beings are autonomous, not heteronomous, and in turn, their autonomy would imply that the ethical grounds for exploitation would cease to exist. In a word, that groundwork would die. And the lives that such a bloodless death would feed!

Fungal, botanical, and microbial beings are well-known affiliates of death and decomposition, but according to Hegel's student Ludwig Feuerbach, we ought not run from death because not only is it inevitable, but as he reasons, death is an act of sharing. In 1830, he claimed that upon death, the consciousness once contained by the living individual is released into the wilds of earthly existence.[7] Boundaries that were once erected around the living capsule decompose, and its consciousness leaks out into the environs, like a wadi coursing through the Sahara in spring, which is then drunk by desert blossoms and thirsty camels—or better, like a raindrop destroyed when it splashes into a bird's nest fungus, but whose energy is redistributed to the peridioles and their spores. For Feuerbach, death relinquishes the hold over one's

---

[7] Feuerbach, Ludwig, *Thoughts on Death and Immortality from the Papers of a Thinker, along with an Appendix of Theological Satirical Epigrams, Edited by One of His Friends*, translated by James A. Massey (Berkely, Los Angeles, and London: University of California Press, 1980).

own gifts, releasing them into the world to be absorbed by others, and in this way, death is the ultimate act of love. So, like these waters, consciousness, personhood or knowledge is distributed and cycled through all things. And in this way, death—whether of a failed idea or a failed body—is productive, generative, and even creative.

The metaphysical question of consciousness, mind, and agency in nonhuman things has regained attention lately, in no small part due to our increased understanding of the varieties of cognition and communication pulsing through the daily lives of invertebrate and microscopic organisms— and even, maybe, subatomic particles. Among philosophers of the continental tradition, speculative realists maintain that agency is distributed, if unevenly, between all things— animate and inanimate, real and imagined. No agent acts alone but, rather like Andy Clark and David Chalmers's famous extended mind thesis, where thought and reason are outsourced to external entities, agency is often external and combined in assemblages, creating what we might call ecologies of will.[8] However, in this position, agency is not akin to consciousness but rather the capacity to exert some influence, whether intentionally or not, over actions and transactions. The bird's nest fungus who awaits the perfect

---

[8]Neatly summarized in Bryant, *Onto-Cartography*, 2021, 74-75. Compare to the continental tradition of vitalism in Scott Lash, "Life (Vitalism)," *Theory, Culture & Society* 23.2-3 (2006): 323-349.

raindrop to launch those peridioles into the air, or all the imperfect raindrops falling in the meantime, may not have the intention of affecting those sticky spore pods; but for the speculative realist, intention is irrespective of agency, which is merely the capacity for causality.

For Kantians, this would be a radical position, but when compared to some Indigenous North American philosophies, it is a hesitant one at best. Anishnaabe and Haudenosaunee scholar Vanessa Watts explains that land is not just an agent or actant, and it is not merely alive. It—indeed, she—thinks and desires, contemplates and wills. Habitats and ecosystems, organized by land and her relation to water and air, are better conceived as societies with their own sets of ethics and values.[9] Human agency and autonomy are merely derivative of the land's first consciousness, just as our bodies are derived from the soil. How strange it is that Indigenous creation pulls human bodies from land in much the same way that the Abrahamic god (יהוה or ﷲ) composed Adam—whose name is derivative of soil in Hebrew (אדמה) and the color of soil in Arabic (آدم)—from the earth, yet in the case of Abrahamic creation, it seems to have served to estrange man from land rather than to reinforce his responsibilities to her.

In the soil that formed the first people, how many millions of hyphae were there squirming into longer and increasingly

---

[9]Watts, Vanessa, "Indigenous Place-Thought and Agency amongst Humans and Non-humans (First Woman and Sky Woman go on a European Tour!)," *Decolonization, Indigeneity, Education and Society* 2.1 (2013): 20–34.

entangled mycelia? How many fungal kinds were represented in those spirited lumps of *adamah*? That soil is weirdly alive and even conscious is becoming more readily defensible from a scientific perspective. Many analytic philosophers too are increasingly defending a kind of panpsychism that acknowledges a universal consciousness from which individual subjects emerge, but to which they always remain grounded. Objects are discrete, individual, and autonomous, but emerge like bubbles from a frothy, mucilaginous source. This theory has the advantage of avoiding the Cartesian mind/body dualism that presents a disjointed explanation for experience and an inadequate explanation for how minds and bodies interact. At the same time, it also avoids the problem of scientistic physicalism where material explanations exist for all phenomena but which cannot adequately explain the evolutionary emergence of consciousness most witnessed in humans, and increasingly recognized in other organisms too.

While panpsychism is parsimonious, an elegant or harmonious theory is no precondition for its accuracy.[10] That

---

[10]Goff, Philip, "Universal Consciousness as the Ground of Logic," *Panentheism and Panpsychism: Philosophy of Religion Meets Philosophy of Mind* eds. Godehard Brüntrup, Benedikt Paul Göcke, and Ludwig Jaskolla, (Leiden: Brill, 2020), 107-122. A good example of how the elegant and harmonious does not necessarily equate to the true is in conspiracy theories. Thanks to Jeremy Killian for sharing his expertise on the aesthetics of conspiracy theories—one feature of which is their all-encompassing explanations that deny coincidence and errant data—with my students and myself over the last few years.

said, the panpsychist's position has the further advantage of correlating with many Indigenous philosophies while also taking seriously the experiences of mystics undergoing intensive meditation or psychedelic transformation. In the case of the latter, mushroom magic has been giving those who dare—the alchemists, Aldous Huxleys, María Sabinas, Mithraic initiates, circumpolar shamans, Aztec sacrificial victims—a glimpse into the very ground of a waking cosmos, a cosmos that quakes and quivers, that is animated and lit up like a cartoon alt-world against a field of dark energy.

As explained above, these mysterious and earthborn psychoactive substances are known to ethnobotanists as "entheogens"—things that possess you with the spirit of a god, or that burst open your mind to universal consciousness. I would like to propose here that we consider the powers of non-psychoactive mushrooms too, along with all their fungal kin, to peel back the layers of elusive reality, like thin sheets of lamellae, and to expose the fragility of long-cherished ontological ideas of human superiority.

This *mushroom metaphysics* is aware of the magic that binds us together; it senses that the cosmos and Earth in it is alive; it remembers the rare, fecund nature of our planet and that our lives are derived from earth and stars; it experiences the greatness of living small; it knows that humans are but one sentient being among so many, and that our vulnerability to infection, death, and rot is part of what makes us also susceptible to the extraordinary pleasures and simple beauties of everyday subsistence; and it implores us to take responsibility for how we behave inside the land and waters who define Earth's contours, and to live by reciprocity. As we meditate on these principles, perhaps we might even expand the concept of "entheogen" to something like "myco-theology."

Instead of lording over from above, shining down from beyond, the chthonic nature of myco-theology doesn't differentiate within from without. The myco-theological subject is the object. It is a being that lurks beneath your feet and behind your shoulders, inside your most private parts, but rarely above your head. With emotions dissimilar to man's, it may not care if you or any other person is living or dead. For this being, there is no heavenward, only earthbound. This being takes you by surprise, like a trickster—Anansi, Loki, Hermes, Set, Raven or Coyote—yet it is neither supreme nor even divine. This being doesn't want your worship or obeisance, your prayers or hymns, or your Sunday best. But you will have to make sacrifices.

Yet these are not the blood sacrifices familiar to the pious. For a myco-theologian, sacrifice is slitting the throat of excess and eviscerating toxic waste. Sacrifice is letting go of consumer impulses and the asinine optimism of capitalism. Sacrifice is doing the hard work yourself without expecting others, whether blue collar or indigo milk cap, to follow behind and clean up after your mess. No blood, no martyrs; no slaves, no masters.

At least part of this kind of sacrifice requires knowing that these aren't really sacrifices at all, or at least not in comparison to those we'll have to make if ecocide continues unchecked. That said, this sacrifice also requires putting in the effort to learn what other pleasures, joys, and wonders there are besides the artificial controls of purchasing power, technocracy, and all the others that function to overwhelm— or to walk *on* Earth rather than *with* her, or, better yet, *in* her.[11] As Timothy Morton summarizes, "consumerism is a terrible photocopy of the kinds of pleasure that a more just society would afford. And the very concept of pleasure within consumerism, the concept derived from utilitarianism, is ugly and flawed."[12] A myco-theologian would of course find nothing intrinsically wrong with being either ugly or flawed, but Morton's point is simply that the flighty pseudo-pleasure of consumerism is the same as that of a greedy god: always wanting more, never satisfied by giving without expecting something in return. By contrast, reciprocity isn't obligatory or utilitarian but acknowledges that others exist on their own terms beyond your personal needs or desires. Respecting reciprocity helps us gift and give back in ways that are meaningful, ways that recognize the superabundance of consciousness among us.

---

[11]Bryant, L., "Wilderness heritage: for an ontology of the Anthropocene," *Heritage Ecologies*, eds. Torgeir Rinke Bangstad and Þóra Pétursdóttir (London and New York: Routledge 2021), 75.

[12]Morton, Timothy, "Inheritance," *Heritage Ecologies*, eds. Torgeir Rinke Bangstad and Þóra Pétursdóttir (London and New York: Routledge 2021), 387.

Falling Stars

Twenty-five years ago, British folklorist Adrian Morgan concluded his brilliant and beautiful volume *Toads and Toadstools* with a lamentation and plea for unity: "We live in anxious times, with political establishments crumbling after long existence as rigid monoliths. Into the vacuum of broken empires have come nationalist and religious movements, whose most extreme members pose a threat to peace." He goes on to say that the planet is experiencing a spiritual crisis, by which he almost certainly meant the human portion of the planet, and he locates the source of this crisis in the loss of a sense of belonging. He explains that

> Most of us have lost touch with our ancestral and cultural heritage, and the rise of many social and political movements reflects this. . . . The larger the societies in which we live, the less we can feel the true sense of belonging that our ancestors must have felt in their small codependent groups. In a quest to belong, many people have reverted to ignorant and xenophobic attitudes of tribalism, religious bigotry, and racial separation.[13]

He points to "patriarchal political and religious leaders who use simplistic versions of 'history' and 'religion' to justify the slaughters and injustices of the present" before offering an

---

[13]Morgan, *Toads and Toadstools*, 192.

antidote: "it is worthwhile to remember [that] cultural and mythic parallels unite peoples of European, Asian, Native American, African, and Oceanic descent." He continues,

> Monotheistic principles may have sound spiritual values, but in practice they often serve to divide societies against anyone who does not fit in with their narrow, and often tyrannically sexist, concepts. If people could look deeper into their past, into their pagan heritage, they would find a wealth of cultural tradition that suggests there is far more to unite the warring factions of humankind than there is to separate them.[14]

It seems likely that Morgan was a nascent myco-theologian. While his more Rousseauian sentiments are debatable, such as the idea that sexism is a product of modernity or monotheism (it definitely is not), many scholars and social commentators of late have remarked on the increasing alienation and anomie experienced in oversized, internet-dependent, workaholic, consumer societies.

Reflecting on his words from the current standpoint of resurging religious authoritarianism and national populism, a viral pandemic resulting from the thrusts of neoliberalism into the furthest reaches of Earth, an unprecedented anthropogenic climate crisis, and the sixth mass extinction,

---

[14]Ibid.

his plea rings truer and resonates further now than when it was first written a quarter of a century ago. While I may take an uncommon position that peace is an overrated and impossible ideal, there is a common, maybe even conscious, ground that unites us nonetheless. Morgan's "spiritual crisis of the planet" suggests that if humans are experiencing such a crisis, Earth and her constituents are experiencing its reverberations, at least.

As we all sense these violent reverberations that send ecosystems into decline, primitivism becomes appealing. It's too easy to glorify pagan, Indigenous, ancient, or otherwise non-Western cultures while decrying the one we find ourselves occupying by happenstance of birth. This primitivist position is not only too easy, but it's also based on misconception. Early humans absorbed our Neanderthal and Denisovan cousins, probably not without unspeakable violence. Our Ice Age ancestors hunted hundreds of Pleistocene megafaunal species to extinction, and then set about genetically modifying plants and animals to supply themselves with a steady source of food and labor. Some pre-contact American kingdoms over-farmed and deforested their territories to the extent that they could not survive prolonged drought. These kingdoms disintegrated or collapsed, often violently. There are countless examples from all human societies of sickening cruelty enacted against fellow people and our nonhuman compatriots. None ever was, and none is, utopian. Because of this, cultural relativism can only bring us so far. Yet so too are clear the limitations of the Enlightenment emphasis on human flourishing, which has excluded even many humans and which has come at incalculable cost to everyone else. Now ecocide rages at an unprecedented scale due to the spread of a few related, parasitic ideologies across the entirety of Earth's surface, her heated atmospheric heights, and plastic-strewn oceanic depths.

While guarding against the lure of primitivism, the apocalypticism of these circumstances means that solutions, and even just hope, are hard to come by. There is a tendency to see the wasting lands, smogging skies, and deadening oceans in the same way that an alchemist might be drawn to putrefaction as a precondition for the "eternal renewal of things in the midst of decay." In a similar vein, there is a Christological aspect to the idea that this Anthropocene is just a phase of destitution or abjection from which we will eventually emerge, redeemed and transcended.[15] On the other side of this Armageddon, our spiritual lives will be better, our CO_2 scrubbers effective, our energy green and clean, plenty of lab-cultured meat for all nine billion of us

---

[15]Noys, Benjamin, 'The Savage Ontology of Insurrection: Negativity, Life & Anarchy," *The Anomie of the Earth: Philosophy, Politics, and Autonomy in Europe and the Americas*, eds. Federico Luisetti, John Pickles, and Wilson Kaiser (Durham and London: Duke University Press, 2015) 174-191. Merchant, Carolyn, "Reinventing Eden: Western Culture as a Recovery Narrative," *Uncommon Ground: Rethinking the Human Place in Nature*, ed. W. Cronon (New York: W.W. Norton, 1996), 132-159.

(and counting), and micro-organisms abound to break down all our toxic wastes. We'll be able to have our cake and eat it too—or, perhaps, we'll be able to have our Communion bread and eat it too.

The monks at Mepkin Abbey, north of Charleston, grow and sell oyster and shiitake mushrooms to support monastic life. The abbey is nestled in a bend of the Cooper River, a former plantation with enslaved workers which is still dotted with ancient live oaks drenched in Spanish moss, still maintained impeccably with gardens and cemeteries (though not of the enslaved), but now farmed by vegetarian Trappist monks who raise vegetables and mushrooms. A fun yet meditative twist is that the grounds also feature a labyrinth. This seven-circuit circular labyrinth is meant to mimic life— the bends and turns, the sense of disorientation followed by reassurance that one is indeed on the right path. At the labyrinth's entrance, there is a sign that quotes St. Augustine: *solvitur ambulando* (it is solved by walking).

As I walked the convoluted pathway, my gaze toward the ground, grasshoppers leapt away from my slow, deliberate footfall, and into the wildflowers that outline willy-nilly the contours of the labyrinth's circuit. The way was punctuated with fire-ant hills and the shouting of crows in the distance. At one point, I spotted the burrow of some cheating rabbit who hit course three and decided to bail and burrow her way out. Who knows how many paces later, and I found her exit point. Good for her. Finally reaching the center, I sat on one of seven wooden stools and closed my eyes. Beads of sweat tickled my spine as they calmly rolled down my back, and the joyful sounds of songbirds seemed amplified from the moss-covered oaks surrounding the labyrinth. In this place, where my values seem to align so well with those of the current residents, differences of faith seemed merely semantic. But as I walked back out, airplanes shrieked overhead, and some big truck blasted New Country through the abbey's lanes, and I remembered, reassured, that there are important differences—and that, indeed, *solvitur ambulando*.

In a recent blog post, Father Joseph Kerrigan writes that COVID-19 pandemic restrictions impeded the monastery's ability to market those mushrooms, the profit from which is a primary means of the abbey's sustenance.[16] Nevertheless, Father Kerrigan finds in their mushrooms a parable to teach the ability of the faith in general and the abbey in particular to transcend such difficult times. The church's altar is like the substrate from which mushrooms grow; scriptures are spores "released into the community to linger for later fruitfulness." Prayer, work, and community are the mycelial network that holds the monastery together, obscurely "converting dead materials in the service of life." Society has regressed, and like foragers, we "are fighting off the wild beasts of selfishness and narcissism" as community is rebuilt around the common

---

[16]Kerrigan, Father Joseph, "Mushrooms Are Us! Mycelian Possibilities for Monasteries and Pandemics," n.d.: https://mepkinabbey.org/mushrooms-are-us/, last accessed 26 December 2021.

purpose of faith. His metaphor reminds me of Stamets and McCoy, who dislocate their faith from the messiah and relocate it to the mycelium. In either case, the world will be rescued by one savior or another, and we will prosper again.

The first problem here is that awaiting salvation deflects and delays responsibility, and the second is that capitalism is designed to suspend the prosperity of the many against infinite, parasitic, growth of the few. Within these two systems, we will achieve nothing, and in the meantime, the blood of sacrifices made will increasingly be contaminated with microplastics.

Always wary of the unintended consequences of capitalism and monotheism, my present antipathy has been especially piqued given that I'm writing at a time of year when plastic angels are enthroned atop evergreen trees, themselves sometimes plastic, hoarding beneath their boughs mass-produced gifts purchased en masse. Bank accounts are sacrificed to fund exchanges that are notoriously perfunctory rather than emerging from love or reciprocity. Houses are lit with colorful, coal-fired electrical lights, twinkling and blinking as if artificial stars had fallen to Earth, a reminder perhaps of the star that led a trio of astronomers to the hiding place of an infant god.

Christmas is a strange holiday, purporting to celebrate that infant god's birth to a virgin, miracle of miracles. In reality, it probably does more to celebrate the god of capital; although as sociologist Max Weber famously pointed out years ago, the latter is something of an aspect or epithet of the former.

But even as politically and religiously divided families come together in superspreader events to overeat, overdrink, and unwrap presents they may not need or even want, there is a certain magic to the holiday that appeals to nonbelievers too. The kitsch and commercialism and decadence are balanced somehow by nostalgic remembrances of times past, simpler times when snow still fell predictably, and when a hot fireplace and a warm drink were sufficient to celebrate the coming of longer days and the hope and rejuvenation that arrive with spring. At least some of that sentimental magic, to Adrian Morgan's delight, may be rooted in the very pagan, and probably psychedelic, origins of the Christmas spirit.

My inquiries into the pagan origins of Christmas date back to when I began studying the Bible with Jehovah's Witnesses as a curious ten-year-old bookworm. With a demonstrated commitment to this new knowledge and the conflict that it presented to my faith, it would be another ten years before I would celebrate that holiday, or any others.

But these days, it's become common knowledge that the time of Christ's birth was placed on the Julian calendar in conjunction with the festival of the Roman sun god Sol Invictus, on what is known in today's Gregorian calendar as December 25. This date immediately follows the winter solstice, which is the point after which days grow longer and nights shorter, when light slowly triumphs over darkness and spring over winter. The two gods, Christ and Sol Invictus, were fully conflated by the fourth century, when Christianity became the official religion of the Roman empire, and the festival was consistently dedicated to Christ's nativity. This explains the timing near the solstice, but where do Santa Claus, decorated trees, and flying reindeer fit into the Christmas miracles?

Do a Google image search for Victorian Christmas cards featuring Santa sitting astride a fly agaric—so much crimson and white trim! In another search, try Christmas tree decorations of a white-bearded gnome atop a fly agaric; these are especially popular in Northern Europe.

In its own Westernized and masculinized way, this imagery references the traditional practices of shamans, the spiritual leaders in boreal forests from Scandinavia to Lake Superior who consume fly agaric as part of spiritual quests. Although the English name for this mushroom refers to its ability to neutralize flies, it happens also to allude to the sense of flying it brings to those who ingest it. The mushroom's psychoactive compound, formerly known as muscarine (hence, *Amanita muscaria*), is harnessed in combination with rhythmic drumming to open the mind and heart to the spirit world, or if you prefer, to universal consciousness. These mushrooms are often found beneath pines, spruces, and firs, like gifts wrapped in glistening crimson and white. In many cases, shamans are joined by reindeer (or in North America, caribou) who eat these mushrooms too, and in their own way, they fly, much like those who pull Santa's magical sleigh from the North Pole on Christmas Eve. Among various Siberian cultures, human and reindeer urine alike is collected and drunk so that none of the mushroom's hallucinatory gifts should go to waste. Reportedly, village shamans may have shared their fungal gifts with households on the eve of the winter solstice by dropping them in through the yurt's chimney when snow packed the door closed. Revelry abounded, and divisions were forgotten. Community was fortified. In a most unusual way, the Mysteries of the mushroom entangle in their crawling mycelial filaments the distinctions between Indigenous and Western religious practices, especially during Christmas. There is surely something magical about all of this.

* * *

In the weeks leading up to this year's winter solstice in the cypress swamps, it's averaged 70 degrees Fahrenheit, climbing up to 80 on occasion. Needless to say, there will be no white Christmas in my near future. Nonetheless, there have been a few days cool enough to run with my Malamutes, Keema and Nanook (we'd prefer a northerly climate, or back to the mountains, but have determined to grow where we've been planted). On those few days, we've bounded through pines and cypresses, the ground soft from the blanket of needles and dry from the low rainfall since spring. It has not been a great year for foraging around here, but even so, the trails have been periodically emblazoned by festive ruby caps with white flecks. But more common to the American South are the orange sorbet-hued peach agaric (*Amanita persicina*) whose pileus is more copper than crimson, more rust than blood. This peach is not angelic sweet like those who grow on trees in the orchards upriver of the swamp; these are earthy, even nutty, both in their flavor and in the sense of being unpredictable like a loose cannon. If you eat it, this peach might just blow your mind and shoot you into an infinite, wondrous connection to every other thing on Earth. Now that's joy to the world!

Back on Waccamaw tribal grounds, the winter solstice was celebrated with the Fire Ceremony, the same way it's been celebrated every year for who knows how long. This happened to be my first fire ceremony with a newly minted tribal ID card, but there will be many more.[17] One by one, we participants were smudged with sage smoke from a seashell, wafted over our bodies with a fan of wild turkey feathers. Now purified, one by one, we entered the sacred circle with a handful of tobacco and cedar shavings. A pinch was offered to the east and then to the fire. Movements were coordinated with each cardinal direction and accompanied with a modest, bloodless, offering. Upon coming full circle, we each offered the remainder of the tobacco and cedar to the fire, and wafted the smoke over face and hair in a cleansing act of humility and finality, before returning to the perimeter of the circle. After everyone had returned, Chief Hatcher spoke of the smoke ascending skyward to the Wakan Tanka,

---

[17]My gratitude to Vice Chief Cheryl Sievers-Cail for nominating me for honorary tribal membership, to Council for their votes in my favor, and to everyone who has welcomed me as a member of the people. I am humbled and honored to be among the Waccamaw.

or Great Spirit of the Sioux, who speak a language related to that of the Waccamaw ancestors, before their dialect was overpowered by the forces of settler colonialism. Chief also named the Great Mystery, and he explained how the fire is a mysterious and powerful gift to humankind, that it radiates the gift of continuity for his people.

But the concept of continuity here is an unusual, unexpected one. These traditional words from a visually imposing Indian Chief, who is also a self-avowed agnostic and a politically liberal Purple Heart recipient for service in Vietnam, came right before the fire-keeper (a role of enormous spiritual importance) showed me his three cross tattoos and talked about getting a new one of a praying Jesus on his upper back. Here in Waccamaw country, continuity is expressed through mutual respect despite fundamental spiritual and political differences.

After the ceremony and before the feast, a plate of food was set out for the spirits in another bloodless sacrifice. The plate was left for crows, possums, and flies to consume, energizing them for cold nights as their scats would be enveloped by the hungry soil and those living there. The spirit plate redistributes energy back into the community of being. And so, for the Waccamaw, continuity means being bound by the membrane of remembrance of ancient traditions that honor even the ontological differences among us, traditions that honor the ancestors alongside the aliveness of all things—or more precisely, the Mysteriousness of all things.

To be sure, mushroom metaphysics is more magic than religion. Unlike the followers and the students, the myco-theologian does not resolve oneself to being mushroom-like. While many mushrooms and fungal kin have admirable qualities, to model ourselves after them would be a mistake. Instead, the responsible practitioner of mushroom metaphysics recognizes difference to envision compatibility. Like many other lifeforms, we can be cooperative, altruistic, generous, and gracious. But most notable among the human talents are those of reason and creativity. With all these gifts, we can be the occasional predators we are without resorting to cruelty, subterfuge, or torture, without delighting in the suffering of our prey, or maybe worse yet, being apathetic towards it. There is no need for us to deny our animal nature or attempt to somehow transcend it; we are animals, plain and simple. But we cannot continue to use our creative intelligence as an excuse for excess, subjugation, and overkill. To form mutualistic partnerships, we need to leave parasitism to the actual parasites—the honey mushrooms, birch polypores, and lobster claws—who do important ecological work.

We have our own ecological work to do, which requires using our gifts—one of which entails the ability to learn the lessons of past and present failures, and the role of faulty ideologies among them—creatively and responsibly, to contribute to the flourishing of Earth and her earthlings. So, for the sake of our fellows derived equally from this magical planet, let's get to work. There are gallows, whole structures, entire systems to be dismantled or burned to the ground.

To be clear, myco-theologically, there will be no peace on Earth, no goodwill to only men. Not even the survival of *H. sapiens* is of particular concern. We are transient; no matter what we do, we will not inherit the earth. That gift of reason has allowed us to think thought's extinction: that is, to know that our species, the last of the *Homo* genus, will die out too.[18] Our extinction may or may not be caused by the current ecocidal global warming hellscape that we have caused. But even despite the eventual annihilation of our own species, we can work, and work hard, to take down as few bystanders with us as possible. That desire to hold dear the frogs and bats, songbirds and corals, snails and whales, sundews and lichens—and to take comfort in the knowledge that life on Earth will go on for a long while with or without us—is at the heart of myco-theology.

This extinction event is a clear confrontation with death and decay. Mushrooms are their harbingers, but so too are they the heralds of strange new lives. Astronomer Martin Beech once wrote, "Signs of decay are all around us and synonymous with such thoughts of earthly frailty is the image of mysterious fungi. The transient flash of falling-stars or meteors reminds us that even the universe is slowly running

---

[18]Rosen, Matt, *Speculative Annihilationism: The Intersection of Archaeology and Extinction* (Winchester: Zero Books, 2019).

down."[19] Questioning the origins of life and the eventuality of death, peoples like the Blackfeet of the Northern Plains, the Tepehuán of Mexico, the Cymry in Wales, and many others have found a causal link between shooting stars or lightning bolts and the sudden appearance of mushrooms, especially jellies, puffballs, and earthstars. Mushrooms are rightly attributed with bringing, distributing, and restoring life on our shared planet, as they always have done.

Guardian angels for some, destroying angels for others, and fallen angels for all, they are fires that spread and wane but never stop burning (*ignis mutat res*); they are new beings who emerge from defecation and decomposition but who never bother to lord it over anyone else. Their kind always drifts from the air back down to earth. The entropy of falling stars and ripening earthstars reminds us that the future is unstable and uncertain, and yet even so, self-organizing principles somehow randomly emerge from chaos, redistributing not just order but also life.

And so, on this myco-theological Christmas—with Comet Leonard creeping across the eastern sky and peach agarics pushing through warm pine needles; Venus, Saturn

---

[19]Beech, Martin, "Shooting Stars and Gelatinous Fungi," *Mycologist* 3 (1989): 144; see also Nieves-Rivera, Á. M. and D. A. White, "Ethnomycological Notes. II. Meteorites and Fungus Lore," *Mycologist* 20 (2006): 22-25; Farstadvoll, Stein, "Mold, Weeds and Plastic Lanterns: Ecological Aftermath in a Derelict Garden," *Heritage Ecologies*, eds. Torgeir Rinke Bangstad and Þóra Pétursdóttir (London and New York: Routledge 2021), 332-336.

and Jupiter in alignment; the increasing humility among humans that we are but star-soil like all the rest—there is a spark, a faint glimmer, of hope that the spores of mushroom metaphysics will be strewn into the air, the water, and the bowels, and that Mysteries old and new will arise with them from the rot and ferment of sacred Earth.

FALL

Lion's mane
Dutch: *pruikzwam*; *apekop*
French: *pom pom blanc*
Latin: *Hericeum erinaceus*

The lion's mane mushroom doesn't look like your typical toadstool. Its Latin name means hedgehog, the French name refers to a cheerleader's pompoms, and one of its Dutch names means monkey head. The other, however, meaning wig mushroom, comes a little closer to what it really looks like: the fluffy whitish beard of a mall Santa who rides a Harley Davidson, and it is approximately the same size. However, it is softer to the touch than a biker beard, and tastes much better.

I have found this mushroom in the late autumn on the Grand Strand of South Carolina (following the Myrtle Beach Fall Bike Rally), growing on exposed oak roots midway up an embankment. They also grow on trunks throughout North America, Europe, and Asia, especially of hardwood trees.

They are considered parasitic, but they usually only feed on dead trees.

When you get your lion's mane home, sweep off any debris with a soft-bristled brush, and then chop it into finger-length strips. After cooking, it has the flavor and texture of seafood. I recommend frying the strips with fresh garlic and lemon, as you would calamari or shellfish. Next time I find it, I'm going to try using the smaller pieces as a meatless substitute for clam chowder and bouillabaisse.

Lion's mane is so large that you may need to preserve all or some for later use, which you should do by freezing rather than drying.

POST-AMBLE

Now, at the completion of our metaphorage, you may have noticed that this book nearly resembles its subject matter. You've read through a structured rhythm, not unlike walking itself, with regularly paced chapters, each in two sections. These rhythmic steps have echoed the act of foraging, but also that aspect of mushrooms that is structured into more-or-less predictable and uniform masses of interwoven hyphae composing a thing of certain size, shape, and flavor, with identifiable spore prints and a certain pattern of behavior among its woodland friends and foes. You've also read through seasons of selective wild mushroom picking that cycle in and out in mimicry (and flattery) of the comings and goings of a few kinds of basidiomycetes whom you might encounter in temperate and subtropical zones of the Northern Hemisphere.

But mushrooms aren't always rhythmic or cyclical. They aren't always predictable, or even identifiable. So how can this book represent the sporadic nature of sporophores? Composer John Cage connected mushrooms and music in a process he called "indeterminacy," which artfully reminds readers and listeners how much of mycorrhizal life, and all life, and all our encounters with other lives, are happenstance. Indeterminate indeed, the mesostics that compose *Mushrooms et Variationes* (1983) are meant to be read aloud, a stanza for each breath:

> very glaD
>
> thE
>
> aN idea in mind
>   They found me
> voIce of god
>
> oNce when
> withoUt
>
> caMe
> undeRbrush
>   thEn hydnum
>
> so that i don't interruPt
>
> couldn't find wAy out
>
> what and wheN
>   Defined
>
> shoUted get out of the way
>   Mysterious

Nine breaths for this specimen of *Dentinum repandum* (now *Hydnum repandum*) whose cap's underbelly has an unexpected tickling of spines inspiring its common name, wood hedgehog. A strange reading for a bizarre creature—but they all are. Part found-word poetry, part oracular mycology, Cage's 75-minute composition is ingenious as it is dry, boring even. Just when you think you've made sense from nonsense, you're sent back down the rabbit hole, seeking desperately to find some meaningful foothold amongst the beautiful jabberwocky.

Instead of replicating this kind of indeterminacy here, I want to close by giving you something like bits of mushroom, some shorter some taller, which are dispersed organically throughout this text. There's a puzzle here to solve, a sneaky little word game, that hints at the mischievous, elusive, and reticent nature of mushrooms. As was said before, there's always something to seek, something hidden to find. But this time, just this once, *non solvitur ambulando*.

Your instructions: for each of the genera named in this book, pick out the first two letters (one side grows taller, and the other side grows shorter). Delete duplicates. Unscramble the remaining letters to find the names of at least 30 different toxins or toxic things—object lessons in anagram form that you, dear reader, will hopefully never have to learn the hard way.

Earth is a Wonderland, rife with beautiful and terrible things; let us always be humbled by her Mysteries, and in our place among them.

INDEX

OBJECTLESSONS

Cross them all off your list.

exit
LAURA WADDELL
BLOOMSBURY

9781501358159

TIME FOR CHANGE!

political sign
TOBIAS CARROLL
BLOOMSBURY

9781501358104

snake
ERICA WRIGHT
BLOOMSBURY

9781501348716

bulletproof vest
KENNETH R. ROSEN
BLOOMSBURY

9781501353024

coffee
DINAH LENNEY
BLOOMSBURY

9781501344350

environment
ROLF HALDEN
BLOOMSBURY

9781501361906

"Perfect for slipping in a pocket and pulling out when life is on hold."
– *Toronto Star*

9781501353352

9781501348815

9781501348518

9781501348631

9781501325991

9781501307409